QUEER/EARLY/MODERN

Q UEER / E ARLY / M ODERN

edited by
Michèle Aina Barale,
Jonathan Goldberg,
Michael Moon, and
Eve Kosofsky Sedgwick

Queer / Early / Modern

CARLA FRECCERO

Duke University Press   Durham & London   2006

© 2006 Duke University Press
All rights reserved
Printed in the United States
of America
on acid-free paper ∞
Designed by C. H. Westmoreland
Typeset in Bembo by
Tseng Information Systems, Inc.

LIBRARY OF CONGRESS CATALOGING-
IN-PUBLICATION DATA
Freccero, Carla
Queer/early/modern / Carla Freccero.
p. cm. — (Series Q)
Includes bibliographical references and index.
ISBN 0-8223-3678-2 (cloth : alk. paper)
ISBN 0-8223-3690-1 (pbk. : alk. paper)
1. Homosexuality—Philosophy. 2. Homosexu-
ality—History. 3. Homosexuality in literature.
4. Psychoanalysis and homosexuality.
I. Title. II. Series.
HQ76.25.F72 2005
306.76′601—dc22   2005027145

For Jody

(AND JAMES, IN MEMORIAM)

Contents

꙳

Acknowledgments

⌘ *Queer/Early/Modern* owes its life to a series of conferences, "The Rhetoric of the Other," held four years in succession and devoted to queer French and Francophone studies. I thank the friends and colleagues who organized these conferences for providing me with occasions for the writing of what would become chapters 2, 3, and 4 and for offering incisive critique and commentary on each.

Two graduate seminars also importantly shaped parts of this work, one in literature at the University of California, Santa Cruz, and one in rhetoric at the University of California, Berkeley. I thank the students in both classes for the many hours of close reading and discussion that inspired my thinking in critical ways.

Chapter 2's first incarnation was presented at the University of California, Davis, at a conference titled "Culture and Materiality"; there, Jacques Derrida graciously affirmed its general direction and, with a few brief remarks, helped me think through the problems of grammar and subjectivity in lyric poetry. Teresa de Lauretis read an early draft; her challenging and thoughtful comments made me revisit my thinking many times. I thank her also for brainstorming chapter titles with me. I presented chapters 3, 4, and parts of 5 in other conference venues, especially at the University of California, Berkeley; faculty in Italian, rhetoric, and the participants in the University of California, Berkeley, Center for the Study of Sexual Culture reading group and inaugural conference contributed tremendously to this work, Albert Ascoli, Michael Lucey, Geeta Patel, and Barbara Spackman in particular.

Chapter 4 appears in somewhat abbreviated article form in *Femi-*

nism in Time, special issue, *MLQ* 65 (2004): 29–47. I owe a debt of gratitude to Margaret Ferguson and Marshall Brown, the editors, for having provided astute and intelligent feedback on the argument of the chapter. The lively and engaged interdisciplinary audience at Duke University who heard an early version of this chapter also gave me invaluable critique.

I tested an early version of chapter 5 first at GEMCS, then at the University of California, Santa Cruz. Srinivas Aravamudan, Anjali Arondekar, James Clifford, Christopher Connery, Wlad Godzich, George Haggerty, Ranjana Khanna, David Marriott, and Marc Schachter all offered encouragement, valuable insights, and criticism. Sharon Kinoshita read every chapter with her historically attuned medievalist attentiveness; I learned much from her comments. I thank the readers of the manuscript—Richard Rambuss in particular—for both their praise and their suggestions for improvement; thanks also to editor Ken Wissoker for the always gracious and informed ways he assisted in its revision. Thanks too to Pam Morrison (who guided me through the production of the book), Cherie Westmoreland (the designer), Diana Witt (the indexer), and others at Duke University Press for their assistance. Robert Miotke read chapter 1 in its penultimate form and contributed to it in vital ways. Margaret Morton contributed the image, *Untitled, 1983*, for the cover. The ambiguity of its gender, the ghostliness of its emergence from a background of red chalk—a favorite Renaissance drawing material—and its sorrowful demand seem to encapsulate perfectly beyond words the tonalities of *Queer/Early/Modern*.

This book could not have been written without the research assistance of two graduate students in particular, Julie Cox and Maria Frangos. Maria especially has played a crucial role in shepherding this book into its final form. Biko and Maji were this book's greatest obstacles in their Basenji puppyhood, but I would not have had the heart to continue were it not for the joyfully queer ways their love enlivens me. I thank their many caretakers as well, without whose labor this project would have languished.

Finally, Jody Greene read each chapter as it was written and carefully tracked my arguments, urging greater clarity and thoughtfulness at each turn. Her prose deeply informs mine, as does her person. I thank her for the many ways she made *Queer/Early/Modern* possible.

1

Prolepses

QUEER/EARLY/MODERN

In "Psychoanalysis and Renaissance Culture"—an essay that for many exemplifies the uneasy relationship between new historicism and psychoanalysis—Stephen Greenblatt asks whether psychoanalysis is an appropriate interpretive technique for reading early modern textuality. The issue, for him, is that "the subject"—understood to be the focus of psychoanalytic inquiry—cannot be said to exist before the social order that produces it. In Greenblatt's view, early modern histories and political economies produce the modern psychological subject that, in psychoanalysis, is taken to be the cause of action.[1] Psychoanalytic interpretation therefore performs a metalepsis on early modernity, belatedly attributing a cause (subjectivity) to what is, in fact, an effect (of culture).[2]

One equally materialist response to the observation that psychoanalysis seems causally belated with respect to early modernity has been to dispute, on historical grounds, a certain conception of the modern subject as the subject that serves as one of psychoanalysis's foundational categories. If early modern European textuality foregrounds the status of the subject as linguistically constructed, contingent, textual, and fragmented, then early modern subjectivity has more in common with psychoanalytic and poststructuralist notions of the subject than it does with the modernity that appears in the intervening period of Western European philosophical and literary discourse.[3] Jonathan Dollimore argues, in effect, that the notion of the constructed subject is precisely what poststructuralism and postmodernity have in common with early (pre-eighteenth-century) modernity:

Of the few central beliefs uniting the various post-structuralisms (and connecting them with post/modernism) this is one of the most important: human identity is seen to be determined by, for example, the pre-existing structures of language and ideology, and by the material conditions of human existence. Thus is the subject decentred, and subjectivity revealed as a kind of subjection—not the antithesis of social process but its focus.

In the early modern period also the individual was seen as constituted by and in relation to—even the effect of—a pre-existing order.[4]

Whether or not this can be said to be "actually" the case, it serves as a useful and productive heuristic device for a particular—and "queer" —reading of early modernity. Among other things, this conceptualization allows the suspension by the subject, and any particular instance of the subject, of a normative gender and its concomitant heteronormatively other-directed desiring orientation. Only a textual, nonunified, nonpsychologized subject could be said to allow for such a suspension, at least within a heteronormative and homophobic cultural context. (For the moment I bracket the question—fully and well explored by many historians of sexuality—of whether or not early modern Europe could be said to be such a culture.)[5]

Similar objections of belatedness could be leveled at queer theory. Queer theory seems, through its techniques of reading, to deploy categorical and psychoanalytically inflected notions of sexuality and normativity that European pre- and early modernity would produce only later, and its theoretical provenance lies firmly within the late twentieth century.[6] Indeed, the reversal signified by the rhetorical term *metalepsis* could be seen to embody the spirit of queer analysis in its willful perversion of notions of temporal propriety and the reproductive order of things. To read metaleptically, then, would be to engage in queer theorizing.

Queer/Early/Modern combines the psychoanalytic and poststructuralist dimensions of queer theory in its thinking through the problems of time and rhetorical subjectivity. In referring to the playful and relatively unused opposite of *metalepsis, prolepsis*, I want to hesitate about the question of temporal propriety in relations among early modernity, queer theory, and subjectivity. On the one hand, I embrace the accusation of metalepsis (with a twist) by pointing to the ways early modern textuality is a product of a kind of queer theorizing. On the other hand, as many current productions of Shake-speare plays demonstrate and as many Shakespearean scholars—some of whom were also early modern studies' first queer theorists—have argued, early modern European textuality proleptically anticipates queer theory and queers modernity. This gesture—turning belated-ness into *avant la lettre*—is a kind of historical corrective, but it does not necessarily take seriously the pieties of the discipline that would require the solemn, even dour, marshalling of empirical evidence to prove its point. To the extent, then, that this work queers historicist imperatives, it does so by means of an implicit critique of historicism itself.

The *prolepses* of this chapter title also refers to the designation as "early modern" of the period of Western modernity formerly known as the Renaissance. That expression suggests that "early on," in other words "before" the modern, there was an instantiation of the mod-ern, and so the early modern comes proleptically to figure modernity (in an examination that is, however, always retroactive).[7] The debate about the "early modern" designation as opposed to the designation "Renaissance" has been tackled at length and for a long time, but I bring it up here to highlight precisely those (ideologically marked and thus significant, for modernity) ways in which the period has stood in for the beginning of modernity, its anticipation, its seeds, so to speak, because those are also what are to be read in the tracing of a queerness that is projected backward to the period and forward from it.[8] I therefore take advantage of the prolepses of the period designa-tion even as I remain agnostic about its temporal referential value.

The slashes between *queer, early*, and *modern* in this book's title, in-articulable though they may be, are intended to interrupt the current notion of the Renaissance as the early modern period and to force a pause on what it means to say that something is historically *early* in our genealogies of Western modernity, as well as to focus in on what is meant by *modern*, and how that term signifies when used in the context of discussions of textuality, subjectivity, and sexuality.[9] The slashes also point to my recognition that in many ways to use the term *queer* and to speak of a *prolepsis of queer* in early modernity is to engage in a willfully modern act, one that would be called perversely anachronistic by some Renaissance scholars, some of whom were my teachers and whose ranks have sometimes included myself.[10]

Finally, the slash between *early* and *modern* also allows me to admit considerable uncertainty about the question of whether what I do in reading queer "back then" has anything to do with "back then" or not. In other words, such reading may finally be a matter of the "mere" juxtaposition of *early* and *modern*. While this sort of critical and analytical juxtaposition could be considered historically illegitimate— and thus also illegitimate in relation to the techniques and theories of historicist literary critical practice in which I was trained—it is a familiar and valid logic in other kinds of analytical practices, especially those, such as psychoanalysis, that attend to the particularity of the articulating subject and the rhetorical effects of language: association, for example, along with others such as condensation, displacement, metaphor, metonymy, repetition, and allegory.[11]

Psychoanalysis, as an analytic, is also a historical method, albeit one denigrated by disciplinarily historicist practices. On the one hand, it argues for an eccentric relation between events and their effects; on the other, it often challenges the empiricism of what qualifies as an event itself.[12] Psychoanalysis affords the possibility of producing a fantasmatic historiography that acknowledges what Karl Marx, Louis Althusser, and Slavoj Žižek observe to be the mode through which subjects live not only their histories, but "history" itself, to the extent that history is lived as and through fantasy in the form of ideology.

In a sense, then, I am also reading "against" history, for the reading I do here at times works counter to the imperative—appearing in many discourses called literary as well as those called historical—to respect the directional flow of temporality, the notion that time is composed of contiguous and interrelated joined segments that are also sequential.[13] This does not, nevertheless, mean that the work is anti- or ahistorical.[14] Here I side with Jonathan Goldberg's comment about the interpretive horizons or limits on reading that apply to two logics, textuality and historicity, which are, for him, one and the same: "The logic of textuality that is the logic of historicity means also that the virtually unbounded possibilities of difference are relatively bound within any textual/historic instance."[15] Furthermore, it would be nearly impossible for a Renaissance scholar to read "without history." But I do argue for the possibility that reading historically may mean reading against what is conventionally referred to as history. Not only do I make use of intertextuality, a mode of figural intra- and intertemporal articulation that might be called "literary" rather than historical, but I also invoke identification and one of its common effects, anachronism, as two intimately related and hallowed temporal processes that make up—like and along with desire—queer time.[16] These analyses proceed otherwise than according to a presumed logic of cause and effect, anticipation and result; and otherwise than according to a presumed logic of the "done-ness" of the past, since queer time is haunted by the persistence of affect and ethical imperatives in and across time.[17]

The *queer* of this collection of critical interventions is difficult to define in advance. Over the past decade and a half, this term, as taken up by political movements and by the academy, has undergone myriad transformations and has been the object of heated definitional as well as political debates. Each chapter here seeks to redefine it or to exploit its relative undefinability, its strategic usefulness as a term that in many situations can be said to elude definition. It is a term that, here, does have something to do with a critique of literary critical and historical presumptions of sexual and gender (hetero)normativity, in cultural contexts and in textual subjectivities. It also has something to do with the sexual identities and positionalities, as well as the subjectivities, that have come to be called lesbian, gay, and transgender, but also perverse and narcissistic—that is, queer.[18] At times, *queer* continues to exploit its productive indeterminacy as a word used to designate that which is odd, strange, aslant; in this respect, I will argue that all textuality, when subjected to close reading, can be said to be queer. Ultimately, if this book can be said to have a position on *queer*, it would be to urge resistance to its hypostatization, reification into nominal status as designating an entity, an identity, a thing, and to allow it to continue its outlaw work as a verb and sometimes an adjective.[19]

Each chapter in this book addresses theoretical and historical issues related to debates in queer theory and in early modern studies; each also juxtaposes readings of "early" and "late" modern texts, sometimes canonically literary, as in chapters 2, 3, and 4, where I discuss lyric poetry and short narrative fiction, sometimes "archival," as in the discussion of the PACS (Pacte Civil de Solidarité) legislation in France, the collection of discourses that together form the text of the "Brandon Teena" case, and Jean de Léry's sixteenth-century ethnography of the Tupinamba in Brazil. The status of these texts as canonical or popular cuts across their generic designations, so that, for example, the lyric is not confined to a high Western literary legacy but includes the popular lyric of rock and roll, and the mundanity of the travel narrative is in some respects elevated to the status of the literary or poetic. Each of these texts is enlisted to articulate a theoretical problem posed by current critical debates in queer theory, feminism, the history of sexuality, history, and early modern studies. The first part of the book—Past, Present—takes a critical approach to a series of problems or issues in feminism and in sexuality studies; it proceeds in the mode of critique by examining the work of others against textual readings and a variety of theoretical concerns in order to deconstruct and reinscribe various histories and problematics. In other words, it performs the work of negativity.

Chapter 2, "Always Already Queer (French) Theory," introduces the problematic of *queer* as deployed in institutional and critical contexts by examining a recent response to the term's use by Donald Morton. Morton criticizes the rise of the queer as an avoidance of materialism that is part and parcel of the "linguistic turn" of poststructuralist theory. I take up the accusation of "immateriality" in relation to the queer, explore the legacy of French and French-influenced poststructuralist linguistic, philosophical, and literary theory in the definition and practice of queer theory, and argue that the indeterminacy of the queer—an indeterminacy eroded from both the right and the left—may in fact constitute its usefulness as a deconstructive anti-identitarian critical and political practice. I return to a moment in feminist academic debates around deconstruction that focused on institutionalization as a way to understand and interrogate the drive to consolidate and institutionalize queer studies. Thus the *always already* invoked in the chapter title refers not only to the way queer theory functions as a deconstructive practice in relation to heteronormativity but also to the way the contours of the debates around *queer* assume the form of a certain earlier feminist problematic as well.

I then turn to the lyric as the paradigmatic instance of the explicit construction of a presumptively heterosexual desiring subject that turns out to be strangely queer and ask what it might tell us about romantic love and its institutionalization as discourse in Western modernity. This, too, is an example of how the always already queer subject inhabits heteronormative and masculinist culture from within, even as late modern instances of the lyric—in this chapter, the songs of Melissa Etheridge—bring this deconstructive insight to the fore through disassembling subject-object relations founded on sexual and gender difference.

Chapter 3, "Undoing the Histories of Homosexuality," looks at the "acts versus identities" debate seen to stem from a passage in Michel Foucault's *History of Sexuality* for the way that it has been adopted or refuted in relation to the historical question of early modern sexual identities.[20] Through a close examination of two essays by the principal U.S. explicator of Foucault for the history of (homo)sexuality, David Halperin, I revisit the narratives of the history of sexuality for the way "modern" homosexual identity and "premodern" sodomitic acts depend on the tacit assumption first that the identity under construction is gendered and, second, that it is culturally generalizable or universalizable in modernity.[21] Thus, for example, I ask the question of what would obtain in the examination of acts and identities in the premodern era if the category of gender were included alongside sexuality, why a universal model of modern homosexuality might be problematic, and what these two questions might have to do with each other.

This chapter also addresses itself to the problem—identified by Foucault—with doing a "history" of sexuality. Such a history, I argue, participates in the very regime that, in pursuing the truth of persons through sex, categorizes and thus also "manages" persons on the basis of (sexual) identity. Halperin enlists a fictional text to make, in his own words, a historical point. He thus proposes to find "archives" in the fiction, to reverse the title of Natalie Zemon Davis's book *Fiction in the Archives*. In my own "literary" reading of Boccaccio's story of Pietro di Vinciolo and one of its subtexts, Apuleius's *The Golden Ass*, textuality resists the project of constructing normative identity in the past, thus undoing the historiographic practice of developing a progressivist account of sexual (or any) normative identity. My argument here is that archiving fiction as history in this manner risks normalizing the deeply unreliable and riven subjectivities articulated through fictions of the speaking/writing "voice" in any period in which this activity occurs.

Chapter 4, "Queer Nation: Early/Modern France," links the PACS

—domestic partner—legislation in France to a long genealogy of the French state's investment in kinship regulation. This chapter also strives to demonstrate what it might mean to analyze problematics of gender, race, and sexuality together in relation to the past. I argue that in sixteenth-century France, in the wake of the discovery of the Salic Law as a forged document, a newly emerging class of state technocrats sought to exclude women from the possibility of succession by developing a scientific theory of genetic transmission restricted to men. Thus, in the interests of phallocracy, early French legists crafted a technology of the state that included a strangely queer theory of reproduction. I go on to look at the way Marguerite de Navarre fashioned a fictional political response to this technology by erecting in its place a theory of female sovereign "parthenogenesis."

The Heptameron's story 30, through its depiction of an incestuous mother-son union that, in its issue, produces the perfect couple as the future of the nation, asserts queer kinship as a fantasy of rule (like the more mundane, phallocratic fantasies of rule articulated in instances such as Werner Herzog's *Aguirre*) and thus also sheds light on the reproductive politics of the state. Here I invoke Claude Lévi-Strauss not as anthropological authority, but as poet of incest, to show how fantasies of kinship express fantasies of the nation. And, because Judith Butler has recently explored one such exemplary fantasy in the figure of Antigone and its legacies in order to interrogate current kinship politics and practices, I look at the way in which female exemplars — Antigone, Lucretia, Marguerite's "widow," and finally Elizabeth I — throw into relief and crisis the technologies of kinship that are also intertwined with technologies of rule.[22]

The final chapter, "Queer Spectrality," marks a transformation in the project of the book by engaging in an affirmative "working through" that is open to futurity. It proposes a model of fantasmatic queer historiography based in recent theorizations and critical elaborations of Derridean spectrality and haunting as historico-ethical practices. To see how haunting might more aptly describe and do justice to the historical and affective legacies of trauma and their implications for political and ethical futures, I turn first to the case of "Brandon Teena," whose rape and murder in 1993 continue to shape queer political movement, queer historiography, and the national imaginary. By recasting the events and their meanings in terms of haunting, I explore how those of us who live on might better honor not only the traumatic memory of the person, but also the ethical and political challenges his or her afterlife pose for the present and the future of queer survival.

The second part of the chapter turns to the problematic of haunting and history in relation to studies of European early modern New World conquest and encounter narratives. The question becomes how, on the one hand, to address the historical trauma of European genocidal practices in the Americas and the radical absences they violently produced, and, on the other, what to make of the strange — one might say queer — relations of desire and identification that obtain, both in certain of these texts of the past and between the present and the (imagined) others of the past. The ghostly form that haunting takes, both for New World scholars and for Jean de Léry, writing at the end of the sixteenth century, is the vision and voice, in the text, of an other or others, hallucinatorily superimposed upon and insisting, persisting, in the present.

What role do queer wishes play in this hauntology? To what ethical imperative do these spectral figures respond, and how might such an openness to haunting guide not only our historiographic endeavors, but our present and future political and ethical practices as well? These are the questions I explore at the end of the book, not so much to "solve" a problem of temporal accountability as to suggest alternative ways to respond to — and survive — the not strictly eventful afterlife of trauma in a just, queer, fashion.[23]

Part One

PAST, PRESENT

2

Always Already Queer
(French) Theory

☙ In a 1996 anthology termed a "LesBiGay Cultural Studies" reader, *The Material Queer*, Donald Morton denounces the turn to *queer* as part of what he calls "ludic postmodernism," a legacy bequeathed to current theoretical approaches by the linguistic turn of poststructuralist theories. In "Changing the Terms: (Virtual) Desire and (Actual) Reality," he accuses queer theory and queer theorists of failing to give a material account of desire, to historicize it, and to situate it in global social relations.[1]

Morton's argument combines many of the complaints that have been voiced about queer theory from positions that call themselves leftist and activist and describe themselves as opposed to something they find pernicious about poststructuralist — or what also sometimes gets called postmodern — theory. In particular, Morton associates the queer with the "immateriality" of other concepts in postmodernism: "In the (post) modern moment, desire has displaced need, the signifier has displaced the signified, exchange value has displaced use value, mode of signification has displaced mode of production, textuality has displaced conceptuality, the meaningless has displaced the meaningful, indeterminacy has displaced determination, undecidability has displaced causality, feeling has displaced knowing, difference has displaced commonality, and so on. So, also, in relation to these complex shifts, *the 'queer' has 'returned' to displace the 'gay'*" (10–11; emphasis original).

Rather than the historically grounded, material identities designated by *gay* and *lesbian*, there is now something ungrounded and immaterial called *queer*, which, Morton writes, "exist[s]" in current theory "in a dimensionless dimension and an immaterial materiality" (13). Morton thus aligns *queer* with the poststructuralist critique of identity that has posed a challenge to progressive U.S. politics since its importation into the academy in the seventies.[2] His argument is one example of the way the queer, and queer theory in particular, have joined the ranks of those postmodernist or poststructuralist theories—usually French—that are seen to have made falsely progressive claims for "discursivity" and for "antifoundationalism" as against a more properly grounded historical materialism.[3]

In the course of his argument, however, Morton rematerializes—in order to revalidate—the queer by turning it into a substantive identity category (for example, on 24–25); further, he insists on the use of *queer* as a title for his anthology, and he works to redefine the term so that it designates something material, a "material" queer. This hypostasizing of the category "queer" is not peculiar to Morton's discourse; queer has become both an identitarian position and a refusal of such.[4] As with many of the terms deployed in the context of identity politics and theory, *queer*, like *gay* and *lesbian*, has undergone a congealment, a turning into something: *queer* has aspired to being. So there are queers now, and there is queer studies (though this latter designation sometimes continues to play with the ambiguity between the adjectival and substantive use of the term). One might even argue that the use of *queer* as a substantive has become predominant, at least insofar as the drive to institutionalize a critique or a field of inquiry tends toward that critique's consolidation into an object of knowledge.[5]

This use of *queer* does not necessarily, pace Morton, distinguish itself radically from *lesbian* and *gay*; rather it often operates interchangeably with these other terms or extends them to include certain forms of heterosexual, transsexual, and transgender identities and bisexuality, which have been perceived to be excluded by those prior terms. *Queer*, whose lack of material grounding Morton laments—in its "return" from an earlier epithetical deployment to postmodern theoretical discourse—has been reinvested with substance in his and others' moves to make *queer* an identity and an object of inquiry. *Queer* is, in other words, being institutionalized. It is now simultaneously an identity, a critique, and an object of knowledge.

Morton rejects the various "identity politics" meanings of *queer*, which he also summarizes. In those identitarian contexts, *queer* may be thought of as a sort of "reverse discourse,"[6] the oppressed minority's revalorizing as positive what was once a derogatory term, or a politically necessary though contingent category of identity that one occupies in part because it already lays claim to one through its injurious force as a homophobic epithet;[7] as an umbrella term that designates more capaciously the community for whom it struggles: gays and lesbians, bisexuals, transsexuals and transgendered people, as well as all those considered sexually deviant in the culture;[8] or even, finally, as the self-designation of a younger generation less willing, perhaps, to carry the albatross of gender around with its sexuality.[9] Instead, Morton focuses on *queer*'s theoretical deployment as a symptom of the shift away from historical materialism toward what he calls "a theoretically updated version of idealism" (10). But what if *queer* is not, strictly speaking, an identitarian construct, but rather a critique? *Queer* might then be thought of as naming a non–identity-based critical cultural and political practice that seeks to resist the humanist rights-bearing claims of collective identities understood to be based in a certain affective and sexual practice and a relation to same-sex object choice: *gay* and *lesbian*. Understood in this sense, queer theory operates as a critique of recent consolidations within the academy and in public culture of identity-based fields of inquiry and political movements that seek to secure humanism's promise of universal personhood for historically and politically oppressed groups of people.[10]

Insofar as it carries within it these traces of a poststructuralist critique of the subject and identity, *queer* exploits an older political challenge concerning the status of homosexuality in social analyses relative to other socially marked subject positions, a challenge I will call, picking up on Morton's term, the accusation of immateriality.[11] Homo-sexuality (written this way so as to include the general domain of sexuality, gay and lesbian identity, and substantive designations of *queer*) is often not thought to be material at all: it is accused of invisibility (unlike the markers of skin color, for example); it does not occupy a designated place in the class structure of the social order (it does not constitute itself as a class in a political economy); it does not rest on a common ethnic and religious heritage or a common anatomical "sex," the way that other juridically consolidated categories in the *polis* seem to do. It seems immaterial, in other words. It is something queer, not quite there but sometimes discernible nevertheless, an uncanniness, a ghostliness preserved in the homophobic inflections of the expression, "the specter of homosexuality."[12]

The move to invest *queer* with positivity, to make of it a kind of essence, may be understood to be a rejoinder to these accusations of immateriality. One response has been to show how categories of sexuality *are* material, how subjects of sexuality are produced and invested with material substance.[13] The epithet *queer*, for example, materializes—brings into being—the sexually suspect body it accuses, and this materialization carries consequences with it.[14] Other responses have included historicizations of sexuality, analyses of the place of sexuality in political economies, and, in a very different direction, genetic research that yields evidence of biological materiality. In short, one can refute the accusation by demonstrating the materiality of the category of the sexual, and thus the homosexual, and thus—so the argument goes—the queer.

Another way to rethink the problem of the designation *queer* is to note the way that Morton's frustration with the (re)emergence of *queer* in theoretical contexts seems to echo some earlier (and ongoing) feminist objections lodged against deconstruction, particularly with regard to the perception that deconstruction disaggregates identity, indeed disables or deconstructs the very ground upon or material with which one would seek to construct and consolidate a subject and a politics based on identity.[15] And yet, in spite of the objection, one might argue that it is no longer possible—at least theoretically—to invoke the identitarian category of "woman" as the subject of feminism upon which to base a movement or a politics.[16] By turning to a moment in Anglo-American feminism's debate regarding the institutionalization of feminism and its relation to poststructuralist critique, I hope to show how the history of feminist theorizing about institutionalization may have something to teach those who puzzle over the designation "queer" and both its deconstructive and its institutionalizing peregrinations through the academy.

Peggy Kamuf, in a 1981 essay, "Replacing Feminist Criticism," raises questions concerning feminist criticism and theory's drive to institutionalize by invoking Foucault's critique of the human sciences in *Les mots et les choses*.[17] Foucault's archeology uncovers the recent invention of man as an object of knowledge as against humanism's trans-historical and universal claims. Thus, argues Kamuf,

> Foucault's own conclusion . . . about the necessary displacement of a man-centered or . . . human-centered epistemology might also give feminist scholars reason to pause and to wonder to what extent their efforts must remain caught as a reflection of the same form of nineteenth-century humanism from which we have inherited our pervasively androcentric modes of thought. In other words, if one can accept the major part of this analysis of how and why Western thought about human forms has taken the shape it has, then can one also conclude that modifying that shape to include its feminine contours will result in something fundamentally different? If, on the other hand, the empirical rectification of an empirical error can only result in yet another form of that error which is the possibility of a totalizing reference to an object — whether masculine, feminine, or somehow both — then what is put in question here is perhaps the idea that feminist criticism can seek to define its object and still practice an effective critique of power structures. (107)

Here, as elsewhere, Kamuf argues, Foucault makes the point that "power has pursued its aim of social control through proliferating institutions"; "these institutions," she notes, "may be understood in many cases as the spatial realizations of the principles of humanistic knowledge" (108). In a similar way, the drive to institutionalize, consolidate, and totalize the queer as a field of inquiry and an object of knowledge in the academy, under the rubric of something like "queer studies," may serve instead those very aims the designation "queer" — in both its substantive and nonsubstantive senses — intended to subvert. Like feminism, it risks losing its force as critique and realigning itself with humanism.[18]

I am thus interested in preserving the productive tension that the word and concept *queer* maintains between materiality and immateriality, resisting the urge to turn *queer* into a substantive category. The anxiety about immateriality — both as accusation and as counter-discursive response — depends, to some extent, upon an ideological obfuscation of the rhetorical dimension of language, the way that *queer*'s immateriality might be said to function materially.[19] What if we were to resituate *queer* away from its cultural referentiality as a position or an identity? Is there anything culturally and politically pertinent about its adjectival or verbal force? I want thus to think about *queer* again in a deconstructive context.

Queer, in its deconstructive sense, designates a kind of Derridean *différance*, occupying an interstitial space between binary oppositions; it is a term akin to Trinh T. Minh-ha's "in/appropriated others" or Sue Ellen Case's "vampire"—an uncanny, undead haunting of the other within but not of the category of the human.[20] It is the inscription of a negativity that nevertheless may be said to have force, to act or be active in a positive sense. *Queer* takes, as its inverted privileged terms, *homosexual* or *gay* and *lesbian*, but rather than occupy one pole (the negatively valorized one) of a binary, as these terms have seemed to do, *queer* moves in the space between hetero- and homo-, normative and non-, in order to reinscribe, by occupying a place within but not containable by, heteronormative phallogocentric logic.[21] This use of *queer* finds its energy from the way the term works to undo the binary between *straight* and *gay*, operating uncannily between but also elsewhere. *Queer*—precisely by marking out the space and time of *différance*—can thus show how the two, gay and straight, are inter-implicated and how they differ from themselves from within. Thus other valences or modalities besides those most commonly understood to be designated by *gay* or *lesbian* would also inhabit the space of queer, not only so-called deviant sexualities (sexual desires and identities such as trans- or bisexual)—which in any case work to render the category substantive—but also that which deviates from the norm as such, the force of that deviation. Meanwhile, *queer* can also be a grammatical perversion, a misplaced pronoun, the wrong proper name; it is what is strange, odd, funny, not quite right, improper. Queer is what is and is not there, what disaggregates the coherence of the norm from the very beginning and is ignored in the force to make sense out of the unintelligibilities of grammar and syntax.[22] Like the trace, it is empirically irreducible but not phenomenal. The queer can thus be thought of as the trace in the field of sexuality.[23]

None of these ways of using the term would give rise, in my understanding, to something called "queer studies," except if one were being playfully adjectival (for example, one might call English departments departments of queer studies). Nor would they give rise to

[handwritten marginalia: What is the Trace?]

anything one might describe as a nation or a territory, one that is said to have boundaries—whether crossed or not—or spaces in the physical, geographic, or institutional senses of the word, spaces that could be, therefore, constructed. The spatial valence of queer would have to be spatio-temporal, as différance is, and its emplacement would be deferred indefinitely. It would be a nomadism of sorts.[24]

It is in this sense that queer theory seems French, and that French-influenced poststructuralist theory is already queer in the U.S. context, whether in the field of textuality or in that of liberal democratic politics. The "linguistic turn" in French theory, represented by Saussurian and post-Saussurian thinkers such as Lacan, Irigaray, and Derrida, not only facilitates the rise of queer theory as a literary cultural practice in the United States, but also lends an "always already" quality to the activity of queering. French theory has, in other words, made possible the demonstration of how tropological dimensions of language subvert the very heteronormativity of Western logocentrism and thus, for example, how desire and identification may be unfixed from their sexually differentiated and opposed oedipal poles.[25] Indeed, *queer* may be said to emerge spectrally in deconstructive critique. This emergence, as Kamuf points out, also entails "a *different* sense of the political, one that does not project the eventual realization of a fully present (appropriated) subject that would be at the same time fully representative, one that is not itself shaped and determined by the version of the subject as self-presence."[26] As such, deconstructivist deployments of "queer" critique—by displacing and opening up to the radical indeterminacies of the future—liberal political constructions of the gay citizen-subject.

[handwritten margin note: Tropological reading is a practice of interpreting the figurative meaning of the Bible]

The activity of queering thus does not necessarily bear a close relation to the question of *gay* and *lesbian*, in part because such an activity turns out to be inimical to the construction of categories of identity. We might say, in Carolyn Dinshaw's terms, that "queerness works by contiguity and displacement, knocking signifiers loose, ungrounding bodies, making them strange . . . Queerness articulates not a determinate thing but a relation to existent structures of power . . . and it provokes inquiry into the ways that the 'natural' has been produced by particular discursive matrices of heteronormativity."[27] Queer theory is not the first or the only critique to perform the work Dinshaw refers to; on the contrary, queer theory, or "queering," is simply the most recent name for the form that a certain critique of heteronormativity takes. If the queer, then, is one way to make heterosexuality appear as a cultural norm, it can be said to act as the interruptive process in the hypostatization or consolidation of identity, by attending instead to inscription and to that which resists being ideologically materialized into the individual.

Deconstruction, then, demonstrates the "always already" of the queer within the legibilities of heteronormativity. Insofar as this norm—fixed poles of sexual difference exclusively aligned according to a subject-object opposition of identification and desire—is performative (a reiterated doing, not a being), deconstruction, notes Kamuf, "remarks . . . an ineradicable force of difference—exteriority, materiality, otherness—within the very relation and the jealous zeal with which the same allies with itself, affects and effects itself in a movement of appropriation that is never simply given in the present but must be performed, posed, invented, or traced" (111).[28] Each repeated instance of the norm, in other words, demonstrates both a will to generality or "appropriation" (because what is repeated is asserted as the same) and the impossibility of achieving it.[29]

A critical genealogy of one of heterosexuality's most powerful discourses, the love song, demonstrates, proleptically, the queerness at the heart of heteronormative culture. The love song is a cultural structure, space, or scene that can be said both to construct and to fix a certain relation of the subject to desire in the Western tradition. It is a genre we would certainly expect to be straight, given a presumption of cultural heteronormativity. But if queerness is understood as a certain effect in and of language, then it can be shown to inhabit, from the beginning, the heterosexual matrix of the lyric address.[30]

Petrarch's *Canzoniere*, or "songbook," is said to have fixed for subsequent generations a set of poetic and descriptive norms for the love lyric. Nancy Vickers argues that Petrarchism's influence is so authoritative that "the contemporary lyric 'I' follows every move we make: it is predominantly gendered as male; its message, for the most part, reminds us of the pain of adolescent love; and its discourse often strikingly appropriates classic tropes of petrarchism." Vickers thus claims a Petrarchan influence on rock, a notion elaborated at length by Maria Rosa Menocal in *Shards of Love*.[31] The tradition Petrarch inherits, notes François Rigolot, posits a certain heteronormative arrangement of gender and sexuality:

> Il ne sera pas déraisonnable de poser qu'en règle générale le discours amoureux s'organise autour de modèles thématiques et formels établis depuis longtemps, en théorie et en pratique, par la tradition essentiellement masculine de la *fin'amor*: les publics masculin et féminin . . . s'attendent à ce que le poème mette en scène un Amant, que cet Amant parle à la première personne de sa situation amoureuse, et que ce soit une Dame qui incarne l'objet de son désir.[32]

> It would not be unreasonable to posit that, as a general rule, the discourse of love organizes itself according to thematic and formal models that have been established for a long time, in theory and practice, by the essentially masculine tradition of *fin'amor*: masculine and feminine audiences expect that the poem will feature a Lover, that that Lover will speak in the first person of his amorous condition, and that it will be a Lady who constitutes the object of his desire. (My translation)

The subject in the Petrarchan lyric constitutes itself in relation to a feminine object. It is the reiteration of the subject in the repetition of a series of lyric stances, the seemingly endless reoccupation of the lyric "I" in relation to the object, that fixes and stabilizes this subject. As John Freccero remarks, the content of this lyric poetry — "the idolatrous and unrequited passion for a beautiful and sometimes cruel lady" — is neither innovative nor original; rather, what distinguishes Petrarchan lyric is its (exclusive) preoccupation with the constitution of the poet himself: "The persona created by the serial juxtaposition of dimensionless lyric moments is as illusory as the animation of a film strip, the product of the reader's imagination as much as of the poet's craft; yet, the resultant portrait of an eternally weeping lover remains Petrarch's most distinctive poetic achievement. . . . It remained for centuries the model of poetic self-creation."[33] That reiteration, or "serial juxtaposition," however, ultimately suggests not a dyadic relation between a subject and an object that is other but a split subject, a subject whose object is the creation of that subject.[34] In the Petrarchan situation this is made manifest by the inscription of fame (*lauro*, gendered masculine) in the name of the beloved (*Laura*, gendered feminine). As Jonathan Culler has noted of the apostrophic address of the lyric, "apostrophes . . . work less to establish an 'I-Thou' relation . . . than to dramatize or constitute an image of the self." "This figure," he notes of the "you," "which seems to establish relations between the self and the other can in fact be read as an act of radical interiorization and solipsism."[35]

Thus what is articulated in the Petrarchan lyric exchange between an "I" and a "you" is a relation of both desire and identification.[36] As such, it converges with what recent theorists of sexuality have argued queers subjectivity in relation to the hegemonic heterosexual matrix (whereby gender, desire, and sex are imaginarily unified according to the identification/desire split)[37] by troubling those categories, such that Laura comes to resemble, not so much an "other" object of desire, but a kind of Petrarch in drag. But—or and, as the case may be— the drag really matters. Insofar as the "you" is necessary to the "I" in the lyric, the ordering principles of differentiation between the two are thus sexual difference and heterosexual desire. We might even say that sexual difference and heterosexual desire have been produced as an effect of the necessary division of the "I" and "you" of the lyric utterance. Nevertheless, the trace of something queer inscribed in the name of the object haunts this scene.

Another place where the deconstructive "nonreturn of the subject to itself"—that ineradicable force of difference within the very relation of self to itself—makes its appearance in relation to sexual difference is in the equally Petrarchan poetry of Louise Labé. The lyric subject reiterated throughout Labé's work is coded repeatedly, thematically, as feminine. The first elegy ironically articulates the predicament of occupying both sides of the subject/object split but only one side of the sexual difference divide:

C'estoit mes yeus, dont tant faisois saillir
De traits, à ceus qui trop me regardoient
Et de mon arc assez ne se gardoient.
Mais ces miens traits ces miens yeus me defirent,
Et de vengeance estre exemple me firent. (ll. 28–32)[38]

It was my eyes, from which I made spring forth
many arrows toward those who watched me too much
and did not guard themselves enough from my bow.

But those shafts of mine those same eyes of mine undid,
And made of me an example of revenge. (My translation)

The confusing (or impossible) syntax of the line where the arrows
and eyes belonging to the subject in turn undo her and transform
her from lethal object of the gaze to poet-lover who laments her
condition of unrequited love articulates the difficulty of a lyric poet
simultaneously occupying both positions and might even be said
to demystify as blatant pretext the gendered split of the masculine
poet-persona in this Neoplatonic schema of what looks like a self-
wounding. The trajectory of the desire described is a boomerang: the
beautiful lady (here both subject and object) shoots arrows from her
eyes that then return to pierce those very same eyes. The point of
identification and desire is the end of a circular movement where
source and end are one. In this passage, there is no agency for the return fire: the poet declares that her own arrows circle back around
to wound her. This is certainly queer material, demonstrating the
impossibility of self-appropriation at the heart of the lyric I's (and
therefore love's) most insistent self-declarations.[39]

Elsewhere a certain grammatical perversion would seem to be at
work in the service of "straightening out" the subject's desire. Rigolot
notes a curious ungrammaticality in Labé's writing around the gender of the word love (*amour*). In sixteenth-century French, singular
love is feminine, except when it is personified as Cupid; then it/he is
always masculine. Rigolot argues that the grammatical deviations in
Labé's poetry result from her poetic self-assertion as a female poet,
from "a female wish to assert her independent persona both as subject of love and as subject of poetry."[40] The second elegy, for example,
contains the lines:

Ainsi, Ami, ton absence lointeine
Depuis deus mois me tient en cette peine,
Ne vivant pas, mais mourant d'une Amour
Lequel m'occit dix mile fois le jour. (ll. 89–92, 113)

Thus, friend, you have been away now for two
months: I am so distressed; I don't live
anymore; I am dying of a [feminine] love

that [masculine] kills me ten thousand
times a day. (290; Rigolot's translation)

Rigolot proposes that the unconventionality of the pronoun is "a
hermeneutic problem, closely related to the intentionality of the
text" (291) and that "love, which grammatically must be expressed
in the feminine, must also be *un*grammatically masculine when, in a
female-authored discourse, the love object becomes a man." He identifies "the dramatic switch from '*une* Amour' to '*Lequel* m'occit' as a
meaningful slip related to the existential problems of self-expression"
(292). He also points out that Labé could have, in somewhat less self-
assertive fashion, used *qui*, which would not have allowed for a gender
differentiation in relation to love. But he contends that Labé wishes
emphatically to blame the source for her death: "He kills me . . ."
These and other examples in Labé's corpus establish her, in his argument, as a female—and feminist—poet denouncing the amorous
abuses of male lovers and poets. Rigolot's argument thus connects this
violent swerve from the rigidity of grammatical propriety to the sex
of the poet/persona/subject of the lyric and to Louise Labé's effort
to establish herself aggressively as a female poet.

Yet the grammatical distortions of love in Labé's oeuvre speak not
only to the gendering of the lyric subject but also to the sex of the
object of desire, which comes to be designated, in these moments,
as masculine. Thus, we might rather say that the poetry forcibly
heterosexualizes the play of desire in the lyric by marking the object of the subject's love as (inappropriately, grammatically speaking)
masculine. Heteronormativity thus violently imposes grammatical
queerness to reestablish the sexual normativity of this female poet's
discourse of erotic desire. In this respect, we would not need to
hypothesize, as Rigolot does, "intentionality" or "existential problems of self-expression" in order to account for the grammatical perversion of love.

Louise Labé's work illustrates some of the potential incoherence
poetically produced through the subject's difference from itself and
thus through the unfixing of some of the subject/object poles of
sexual difference in the Petrarchan lyric tradition, even as such "difference" demonstrates itself to be, to a certain extent, a masquerade

of the same. Indeed, the lyric love poetry cited here shows us to what extent "the heterosexual matrix proves to be an imaginary logic that insistently issues forth its own unmanageability."[41]

What happens when, in a modern instance of the love song, the lyric exchange of "I" and "you" does not occur within a grammatically marked heterosexual matrix? I am referring to the songs of rock singer/songwriter and musician Melissa Etheridge. Vickers and Menocal, as I mentioned, argue that rock is the modern popular genre most closely resembling and inheriting the Petrarchan lyric tradition, both thematically and tropologically. It is also a domain rarely acceded to by female musicians, since they characteristically occupy the ventriloquized role of phenomenal "voice" in popular musical forms and thus belong more often to the genre of "pop." This is another reason Etheridge is particularly interesting. If we think of Labé's predicament, we might ask, how does a female vocalist successfully achieve the status of rock lover/poet in the genre? Does she write/sing "as a woman" or "as a man," to phrase the question one way; and to phrase it another, what happens to the (hetero)sexual difference of the lyric address?

Etheridge's early albums obsessively repeat the I/you scene of the lyric: almost every song on the first album involves this apostrophic construction. According to Chris Nickson, author of an unauthorized biography of Melissa Etheridge, Etheridge's lyrics are deliberately "genderless."[42] These lyrics, with their radically unmarked positionalities, seem at times so incoherent as to produce syntactical unintelligibility. Whereas in Labé's lyric economy, the alternation of identification and desire is mediated by the love object as rival subject (the object is also a poet), Etheridge's lyric mediation, between the I and the you, is a rival "she." Combined with the phenomenalization of the singing voice, this triangulation might suggest heterosexual difference within a presumed referential framework of heteronormativity. Yet the inability of the syntax to cohere, except through the phenomenalization of voice, foregrounds the disaggregation of heteronormativity that already queers the lyric from within — undoing that fictitious referential unity of gender, desire, and anatomical sex. And although we "know" now that Melissa Etheridge is a lesbian and thematically we can read back into the lyrics the articulation of a lesbian desire, the queering here is not identity-producing:

> Silence is the steel that pierces and cuts me to the bone
> In dreams the hand that touches you is mine and mine alone
> Cruel is the light is the morning shining down on me
> Hours with the Devil to understand just what you need
> So I wake in the street and I call out your name
> Shout to the sky come on
> Come on let it rain
>
> . . . . .
>
> Just inside the distance I hear the late September dogs
> And so I beg for sleep the child who walked before she crawled
> Damn my soul that remembers and clutches to this pain
> The spear in your side is me[43]

> Pounding heart inside my chest I'm screaming
> I want you, I want you, I want you, I want you
> With your heart in your fist
> You laugh at my situation
> Tell me is it blood that you want
> Then take me strip me cut me see I'm bleeding.[44]

In these fragments, not only are the subject and object unmarked in terms of gender, the very distinctions between the subject and object seem at times difficult, if not impossible, to discern. For example, while initially "silence" is the steel that pierces and cuts "me" to the bone, by the end of the song, the spear in "your" side is "me." In "I Want You," "your" heart is in "your" fist, but if "you" want blood, then "take me strip me cut me see I'm bleeding," and the bloody operation of heart removal threatens to take place in another's body. Both of these fragments invoke monstrous metamorphoses around acts of cutting: it is as though, in the absence of marked gender binaries and heterosexual desire—the heterosexual matrix of intelligibility—difference itself becomes a cutting, a slash between I and you, pure difference, difference as material trace.[45]

Another song, "No Souvenirs," presents similar difficulties of intelligibility with regard to the subject and object of the lyric exchange; this time, however, one of the positions—we cannot tell which—is inscribed with a masculine name, the vexed name of the lover par excellence, Romeo.

> Hello, hello this is Romeo
> Calling from a jackpot telephone
> Shame shame but I love your name
> And the way you make the buffalo roam
> Oh fly, fly I guess this is good-bye
> Oh you packed up your heart
> And you left no souvenirs
> [Chorus:]
> But if you want me you can call me
> In the night you know where I'll be
> . . . . .
> Burn the pictures break the records
> Run far away to a northern town
> Sell your fear and leave me standing here
> With no souvenirs
> . . . . .
> You forward your mail
> You're growing your hair
> You don't want to know where
> I'm calling you from
> Or how come.[46]

Is Romeo the "you," calling from a payphone after having run far away to a northern town, leaving "me" standing here with no souvenirs (but "you" know where "I'll" be in the night if "you" want "me," and "you" can call "me" there)? Or is it "me," and still "you" don't want to know where "I'm" calling from (after I've already told you), or how come. And Romeo (or Juliet?) loves the shame name (of Montague, or Capulet?). This highly eroticized, masculine position in the lyric exchange belongs to which one: the subject or the object? Does it matter?

Another song, "I Really Like You," from *Your Little Secret*, functions similarly and describes explicitly the collapse of, or indistinguishability between, identification and desire:

> I'll buy you mangos baby
> your favorite fruit

I'll shave everything baby
I'll press my suit
I'll find that song by Perry Como you like to sing
I'll eat your TV dinners
And wear your cigar ring
[Chorus:]
Do you think that I can persuade
Don't make me fade because
I really like you baby
I want to see you baby
I really like you baby
I want to be you baby
I'll gladly make you
my first tattoo
you and me forever
in red and black and blue
I'll let you drive my car
I'll even paint my eyes
forget about all my friends
and tell outrageous lies.[47]

In this song, the genders of "I" and "you" are deliberately played with, so that conventionally gender-marked activities such as shaving, painting one's eyes, wearing suits, wearing (cigar) rings, letting someone drive one's car, and tattooing the name of one's beloved on one's body are unmoored from gender determination and juxtaposed, but not lined up on predictable sides of a binary, so as to highlight their properties as belonging to members of either or both sexes. The culminating desire in the song is named as identification: "I want to be you baby." This telos—and I think one can argue that coming as it does at the end of the refrain and comprising the last line of the song, it does indeed constitute a telos of sorts—risks returning homosexual desire, especially female homosexual desire, to the mechanism of narcissistic identification and thus effacing, again, the specificity of desire between women,[48] but we might also say that it gives the lie to the homosocial fiction of the traditional love lyric address to suggest that love (and more especially perhaps, love poetry)—through the alternation of desire and narcissistic identification—does not so readily organize itself within an oedipal scenario that would fix and determine the forever barred and distinct directions of a subject's desire and (her) identification.

Is this that other economy, an economy of abundance, as Irigaray might suggest: "Exchanges without identifiable terms, without accounts, without end" ("Echanges sans termes identifiables, sans comptes, sans fin")?[49] Or is this a place where "the thought of sexual difference within homosexuality" might be theorized in at least some of its complexity?[50] *Never Enough*, Etheridge's first album to go platinum, which is also the first album to feature a song about the subject as rock star ("It's for You"), sports *ME* on the cover. And indeed, once she says *Yes, I Am*, the title of her post–coming out album, it turns out to be immaterial (in terms of what everyone was afraid of)—or rather, it turns out to turn a profit. Thus here, as against some of the claims Morton makes, queerness, rather than the specificity of being lesbian or gay, successfully evades a certain capitalist consumer logic; its very troubled or elusive relation to materiality also does not allow it to settle into commodity fetishism as the thing-ification of a social relation. Once "she" comes out, identifying her self—"she's a lesbian"—what was queer is commodified, made available for profitable circulation and consumption, and settles back ideologically into the undisturbing divide of an identitarian difference that is really not much of one at all. We can perhaps again "safely" say, "Ah, that's hetero," "Ah, that's homo." But the subversion that occurs at the level of the letter is more unsettling, ghostly, queer.

Are we thus to conclude that the Western love song is always already queer and that we have only to deconstruct heteronormative culture for these differences within to appear to displace and estrange the subject of heteronormativity from itself? Yes, and yes. For the very impossibility of fully self-present meaning, of the subject's self-presence to itself, opens the possibility of an other meaning, "a relation to and within difference(s)"[51] and thus of a differently imaginable future, a future whose imaginability is figured by the utopian designation of "queer."

Kamuf asks, "What if . . . one could point up traces of an outside-of-opposition, marks left on the structure of opposition which could only have come from a space exceeding that structure?" She notes that "without such a force, if, in other words, the oppositional structure were totalizable, it would also be utterly immobilized and immobilizing. It would spell the death of any possibility for political . . . change."[52] Thus queer/French theory does indeed envisage the political as its horizon, just as queer politics thrives in France. But if politics requires the deployment of oppositional strategies, or even the strategic essentialism Gayatri Spivak once recommended for identity politics,[53] it is nevertheless just as crucial that a space be kept open for that dislocation of the nonopposable other, a dislocation difficult to achieve in the seemingly progressive effort to institutionalize *queer*, on the one hand, and the more conservative rejection of its nonidentitarian indeterminacy in Morton's call for a grounded and material *gay*, on the other.

3

Undoing the Histories of Homosexuality

If one of the things an analysis of early modern lyric produces is a queered understanding of the subject, an understanding made explicit in some late-twentieth-century productions of the lyric first person, then perhaps alternative histories might be generated to account for and critique heteronormativity's seemingly long-standing regime in the West. Perhaps, too, alternative, queerer, more fantasmatic approaches to history—some of which, in this chapter, I call literary—need to be developed in order to read these legibilities that are neither necessarily visible nor discursively articulated as descriptive accounts of what "is" in pre- and early modern culture.

This chapter seeks to explore and critique what might be occluded in historicist approaches to the past that either do not read what are commonly called fictional or literary texts and discourses, or read them "as" and "for" the historical information they (often deceptively) seem to provide. I argue here against a certain doing of the history of homosexuality that either taxonomizes identities (a historicist project that, in my view, runs counter to Foucault's call for genealogies and archeological projects, even if it is often also done in his name) or wants to account for a preemptively defined category of the present ("modern homosexuality") by developing progressive historical accounts of the evolution of that category. I use the work of David Halperin as an example principally because he has been, to some extent, an exemplary new historicist advocate of "altericist" views of the past and because, in the work I focus on, he chooses a literary example from the Renaissance to make an argument regarding the historical development of "homosexual identity" in the West. Further, he does so in the name of elaborating upon Foucault's project in the *History of Sexuality*, whereas, in my view, it is precisely to counter historicist articulations of the past that Foucault sometimes writes. This is not to say that Halperin's "histories of homosexuality" are wrong; rather, it is to articulate—again—what might occur in a queering of historiography, a queering that, in this instance, comes into being through the deviation of "the literary."

Finally, as part of my own project of coarticulating sexuality and gender as historical and analytical legibilities, I focus on a critical historicist project that, as a function of its claims about modernity, seeks to decouple sexuality and gender. While I am to a degree sympathetic to the political project I believe this impulse to represent, I want to continue to note and, indeed, insist upon both the ways the two demonstrate their constitutive inseparability and the analytical, political and perhaps (who knows?) historical blind spots their analytical separation incurs.

Foucault, Halperin, and the Premodern Sexuality and Gender Debates

Winner of the 1999 Crompton-Noll Award for the best essay in lesbian, gay, and queer studies in the modern languages, "Forgetting Foucault" is an essay—now a chapter in a book—that admonishes the tendency in histories of sexuality to reduce Foucault's discussion of the nineteenth-century "invention" of the homosexual to the declaration that premodernity defined sex acts juridically, whereas modernity ascribes to the individual something called a sexuality, an identity or orientation that is sexually defined and that, when examined, is thought to reveal the truth of the individual.[1] "Forgetting Foucault" is thus Halperin's salutary intervention into the "acts versus identities" debate generated among historians and theorists of sexuality—as a result of a single and, Halperin argues, commonly misunderstood passage—that has enjoyed a long life in part through reference to Halperin's own project in *One Hundred Years of Homosexuality*. He succinctly summarizes the dominant interpretation of the debate: "In the pre-modern and early modern periods, so the claim goes, sexual behavior did not represent a sign or marker of a person's sexual identity; . . . Whence the conclusion that before the modern era sexual deviance could be predicated only of acts, not of persons or identities" (28/96). While for many modernists this has not seemed a problematic claim, for scholars of the premodern it has been a subject of intense debate. Some have questioned the salience of the distinction, noting that identities can be said to be made by acts.[2] Others contend that something like a sexual identity has existed transhistorically in Europe, an argument that many have understood to be essentialist in its bid for a universalist model of sexual sensibility, if not sexuality.[3] Still others have set out in part to demonstrate the existence in premodernity of identitarian categories organized around sex.[4]

Foucault's reference to premodernity in the passage focuses only on "ancient civil or canonical codes" and therefore restricts itself to articulating what "sodomy" was in terms of the law:

La sodomie—celle des anciens droits civil ou canonique—était un type d'actes interdits; leur auteur n'en était que le sujet juridique. L'homosexuel du 19e siècle est devenu un personnage: un passé, une histoire et une enfance, un caractère, une forme de vie; une morphologie aussi, avec une anatomie indiscrète et peut-être une physiologie mystérieuse. Rien de ce qu'[il] est au total n'échappe à sa sexualité . . . Il ne faut pas oublier que la catégorie psychologique, psychiatrique, medicale de l'homosexualité s'est constituée du jour où on l'a caractérisée . . . moins par un type de relations sexuelles que par une certaine qualité de la sensibilité sexuelle, une certaine manière d'intervertir en soi-même le masculin et le féminin. L'homosexualité est apparue comme une des figures de la sexualité lorsqu'elle a été rabattue de la pratique de la sodomie sur une sorte d'androgynie intérieure, un hermaphrodisme de l'âme. Le sodomite était un relaps, l'homosexuel est maintenant une espèce.

As defined by the ancient civil or canonical codes, sodomy was a category of forbidden acts; their author was nothing more than the juridical subject of them. The nineteenth-century homosexual became a personage—a past, a case history, and a childhood, a character, a form of life; also a morphology, with an indiscreet anatomy and possibly a mysterious physiology. Nothing in his total being escapes his sexuality . . . We must not forget that the psychological, psychiatric, medical category of homosexuality was constituted from the moment it was characterized . . . less by a type of sexual relations than by a certain quality of sexual sensibility, a certain way of inverting the masculine and feminine in oneself. Homosexuality appeared as one of the forms of sexuality when it was transposed from the practice of sodomy onto a kind of interior androgyny, a hermaphroditism of the soul. The sodomite was a temporary aberration; the homosexual is now a species.[5]

Foucault does not, in this passage, clarify the distinction Halperin goes on to make between the juridical definition of a sex act and "popular attitudes or private emotions" (29/97), and thus it is not surprising that modernists, in their desire to believe that the past's categories were somehow simpler than those by which we live today, would unproblematically deploy the premodern-versus-modern acts/identities distinction and thereby elide the specificity of Foucault's reference to the law.[6] Indeed, the comparison Foucault makes here between a single discursive domain—the juridical—and a host of nineteenth-century institutional discursive constructions that includes psychology, sexology, education, law, and medicine might itself be read as the symptom of a modernist desire to simplify premodern discursivity by privileging the juridical over other discourses perhaps more obscure and less legible for being less assimilable to modern institutions and discourses. Or it might ultimately have been a mere accident of source availability—whereas the nineteenth century leaves behind a more visible and legible paper trail, the European "dark" ages are shrouded in obscurity and do not yield their data so readily to the historian or genealogist. Or, as Didier Eribon points out, one might say that Foucault did not make much use of nonofficial sources at all, even in the context of the nineteenth and twentieth centuries.[7]

Foucault is making a larger historical argument regarding the construction of new species of individuals through an elaboration and implantation of perversions—what Halperin calls a "distinctively modern method of sexual control" (30/97–98). Thus, Halperin concludes, "Foucault is analyzing the different modalities of power at work in premodern and modern codifications of sexual prohibition, which is to say in two historical instances of sexual discourse attached to institutional practices" (30/98). The point that he makes here is that Foucault is not concerned with specifying identities or practices but is, rather, analyzing changing official discourses and their different modalities of power.

Eribon has since questioned this famous passage on acts and identities in Foucault's *History of Sexuality* from a different angle, that of textual exegesis. In arguing for the continuities (and contradictions) between Foucault's project in *Histoire de la folie* (*Madness and Civilization*) and the later *Histoire de la sexualité*, Eribon points to an ambiguity in Foucault's dating of the emergence of the homosexual as a category of person (*Histoire de la folie* cites the seventeenth rather than the nineteenth century).[8] This would seem to suggest both the importance of the question of the emergence of homosexuality—because, in Eribon's reading, Foucault was already concerned with it in *Histoire de la folie*—and the nonfinality of the later statement in *Histoire de la sexualité*. Eribon's speculative meditation provides an intellectual, political, and historical context for this move—having to do with current events of the sixties and seventies in France, the advent of the FHAR (Front Homosexuel d'Action Révolutionnaire), and the appearance of Guy Hocquenghem's work.[9] Eribon suggests that Foucault may have been reacting against the new militant politics of homosexuality (and the imperative of coming out) by attributing the invention and emergence of homosexuality as an identitarian regime of truth to institutionalized discourses of power-knowledge (in this case, nineteenth-century psychiatry).[10] Thus, by shifting the date of homosexuality's invention, Foucault would have been cautioning against the adoption of homosexuality as a positivist identity category by Hocquenghem and others.

Halperin states that "the case of homosexuality" is but an example of a more general argument regarding the discursive construction of sexual perversions as a way to normalize embodied subjects ("Want an example? Take the case of homosexuality" [31/99]). But homosexuality and, more specifically, male homosexuality is not just one example that can be generalized to other deviant sexualities, but the case where Foucault's argument seems to work the best (Eribon, for instance, implies that homosexuality—Foucault's own—is what he may have been thinking about all along). Eve Kosofsky Sedgwick, Karma Lochrie, Ruth Mazo Karras, and others have suggested that if gender as a mode of materialization inextricable from sexuality had been more fully taken into account, a different picture might have emerged, one that would have shown a tendency in premodernity—as in modernity—to produce particular normalized embodied subjects through a discursive implantation of perversions.[11] Those embodied subjects are the ones we designate by the gender/sex reference *women* or *females*. It would thus have been the very restriction of sexual practices to juridically prohibited sexual behavior that would have identified the subject of those acts as male, because for women acts immediately exposed them as a "personage" understood much the way Foucault argues the nineteenth century understood the homosexual:

> Rien de ce qu'[il] est au total n'échappe à sa sexualité. Partout en [lui,] elle est présente: sous-jacente à toutes ses conduites parce qu'elle en est le principe insidieux et indéfiniment actif; inscrite sans pudeur sur son visage et sur son corps parce qu'elle est un secret qui se trahit toujours. Elle lui est consubstantielle, moins comme un péché d'habitude que comme une nature singulière.

> Nothing in [her] total being escapes [her] sexuality. Everywhere in [her] it is present: underlying all [her] actions, because it is their insidious and indefinitely active principle; shamelessly inscribed on [her] face and on [her] body, because it is a secret that always gives itself away. It is consubstantial with [her], less as a habitual sin than as a singular nature.[12]

What this suggests, in fact, is that the discourse of women in premodern Europe (and, I would argue, in its modern Western Euro-American inheritance) partakes more of Sedgwick's characterization of "minoritizing" and "universalizing" discourses which, in potential at least, coexist and are available for differential mobilization at certain times and in certain places. Sedgwick speaks of transhistorical contradictory discourses around the distinction between heterosexuality and homosexuality; the contradiction, as she frames it, is "between seeing homo/heterosexual definition on the one hand as an issue of active importance primarily for a small, distinct, relatively fixed homosexual minority (. . . the minoritizing view), and seeing it on the other hand as an issue of continuing, determinative importance in the lives of people across the spectrum of sexualities (. . . a universalizing view)."[13]

Karras, for example, writing about the medieval *meretrix* or female prostitute, argues that, on the one hand, the meretrix was a specific type of woman characterized by an irredeemably sinful sexuality and thus was unlike the wives and mothers of patriarchs; and, on the other, all women harbored within themselves a latent meretrix, and any act or behavior resembling that of the meretrix would suffice to realize this latency and enable their repudiation or worse. As she remarks, "All . . . women risked falling into the category of whore. . . . The (minoritized) prostitute thus was a paradigm for the (universalized) lustful woman."[14] Karras illustrates precisely Sedgwick's argument that the two discourses, minoritizing and universalizing, coexist in an "unrationalized," that is, conflicting and contradictory, fashion wherever such models may be said to coexist.[15] She thus demonstrates that the two discourses do in fact coexist; the numerous examples of saints' lives where prostitutes undergo conversion, as well as contemporary sources that argue for the possibility of rehabilitation, demonstrate the potential porosity of the category (166). A woman in the Middle Ages could, in other words, both fall into and rise out of the category of "meretrix." What was required for the latter transformation was the extreme performance of conversion. This argument converges with recent studies of medieval racialization, whereby racialization could also be seen to operate according to the dual nonlogic of minoritizing/universalizing discourses: for the medieval West, a "Saracen" was both profoundly other and at the same time capable of conversion, which rendered him or her indistinguishable from Christians.[16] "Whores," then—and "witches," too, perhaps—are a specific and identifiable category of being. At the same time, however, their existence serves to mobilize powerful misogynist discourses and practices that universalize the sexual deviancy of some women as the reigning attribute of all the daughters of Eve.[17]

In *Epistemology of the Closet*, Sedgwick performs a critique of both Foucault's and Halperin's genealogies of homosexuality that entails targeting, on the one hand, their "narratives of supersession"—the notion that one model of same-sex relations supersedes another, which is in turn superseded by another—and, on the other, the linkage of that supersession in Halperin to a shift from a gender-transitive model of homosexuality (Foucault's androgyne or hermaphrodite as the form in which homosexuality first enters the records of medicine and psychiatry) to a gender-intransitive one (Halperin's model of the "modern" homosexual, where gender and sexuality are detached).[18] Thus the notion that the existence of a discursive regime associated with modernity necessarily entails the disappearance of another, here associated with premodernity, may obscure the particular ways in which multiple and contradictory discourses create tacitly conflictual definitional fields and may indeed "risk reinforcing a dangerous consensus of knowingness about the genuinely *un*known."[19] As for the second problem—Halperin's desire to see, where Foucault does not, gender intransitivity as a defining principle of "modern" homosexuality—this is precisely where the historical analysis of a certain globalized modernity may be seen to break down.

In "Forgetting Foucault," Halperin provides the example of the *kinaidos* as an explicit contrast to modern understandings of homosexuality. Building on his own work on antiquity and that of John Winkler, Maud Gleason, and Craig A. Williams, Halperin argues that (1) "The ancient conception of *kinaidos* . . . depended on indigenous notions of gender" (33/100); and (2) "whatever its superficial resemblances to various contemporary sexual life-forms, the ancient figure of the *cinaedus* or *kinaidos* properly belongs in its own cultural universe. It represents an extinct category of social, sexual, and gender deviance" (103).[20] This leads him to conclude, taking Sedgwick's critique into account, that "the *kinaidos* has not as yet brought us quite into the realm of deviant sexual subjectivity. For whether he was defined in universalizing or minoritizing terms, the *kinaidos* was in any case defined more in terms of gender than in terms of desire" (103), and therefore "unlike the modern homosexual . . . the *kinaidos* was not defined principally by his sexual subjectivity" (38/104).[21] Halperin's own work, he says, demonstrated that the kinds of sexual identity in the ancient Greek world "tended to be determined by a person's gender and social status rather than by a personal psychology" (104; omitted from book). In the later essay, "How to Do the History of Male Homosexuality" (which constitutes the final chapter of the book), Halperin modulates this argument in part by retracting the narrative of supersession in favor of models of "evolution," "accumulation," "accretion," and "overlay": "Their separate histories [the histories of male homosexuality] as well as the history of their interrelations have been obscured *but not superseded* by the recent emergence of the discourses of (homo)sexuality. In fact, what homosexuality signifies today is an effect of this cumulative process of historical overlay and accretion."[22] He concedes Sedgwick's hypothesis of an "unrationalized coexistence of different models of sex and gender in the present day"[23] and argues that this is the result of our inheritance of "pre-homosexual models of male sexual and gender deviance, which derive from a premodern system that privileges gender over sexuality, alongside of (and despite their flagrant conflict with) a more recent homosexual model derived from a modern [*How to Do the History*: "a more recent, comparatively anomalous"] system that privileges sexuality over gender" (109/91).[24] And although this later essay loses some of the confidence with which "Forgetting Foucault" invokes "the modern homosexual," it nevertheless continues to insist upon "what we now call homosexuality" (121/101) as, in Sedgwick's words, "a relatively unified homosexuality that 'we' do 'know today.'"[25]

Can it be said that sexuality constitutes a unitary discursive regime, even in modernity? Hortense Spillers has argued that sexuality as a discursive system—for all its productivity as a dominative mode—"describes another type of discourse that splits the world between the 'West and the Rest of Us,'" thus suggesting—in Foucauldian fashion—that there may be discursive "uneven development" within modernity itself concerning sexuality's reach as a discourse of the truth of sex and sex as the truth of the individual.[26] Elizabeth Grosz also makes this point when she says that "there is no representation of lesbians *as* lesbians in certain key discourses (especially legal and medical) that are deeply invested in power relations," although her conclusion is that the urge to articulate and elaborate such a discourse of female sexuality should be resisted.[27]

Ever since Johannes Fabian's *Time and the Other*, scholars have been aware of the tendency to render cultural difference in terms of temporality; the other of the anthropologist's gaze is likened to an earlier, more "primitive" version of the modern (Western, cosmopolitan) subject.[28] A similar, but reversed, tendency exists today among historians of the premodern (and that tendency is directly related to the incorporation of cultural anthropology into the disciplines of premodern and early modern cultural studies): temporality is spatialized into cultural difference. The effects—political and analytical—are similar. Thus Halperin's description of premodern sexual

identities frames them in terms that suggest radical cultural difference from a modern identity that is "known" to its (modern) con-
temporaries.

Whatever this distinction says about the premodern, it also ho-
mogenizes modern sexual subjectivity by universalizing a U.S. (or
Euro-American) model of gay identity across national, cultural, and
spatial boundaries. By projecting cultural difference onto temporality, this description of historical difference runs the risk of a kind
of ethnocentrism in its characterizations of gay identity.[29] Lisa Rofel
makes this point in her critique of Dennis Altman's "Global Gaze/
Global Gays," which discusses the globalization of gay identity in
China.[30] Rofel asks, "What kinds of investments lead to the assumption that such a subjectivity—a global gay identity—exists?" (453),
noting that Altman "places different sex/gender orders in Asia on a
continuum from tradition to modernity . . . placing the forms that
are culturally marked for him into the category of the traditional
and the ones that approach what he conceives of as 'Western-style'
into the category of the modern" (454). This "modern" identity is
what then comes to be designated as global. Like Halperin, Altman
assumes to a certain degree the self-evidence of modern gay identity, but when he does define its content, it resembles, as we might
expect, that very identity that Halperin implicitly and at times explicitly associates with modern homosexuality: "It contests sexual
rather than gender norms; replaces the idea of male homosexuals as
would-be women with new self-concepts; leads to primary homosexual relationships rather than to marriage with homosex on the
side; expresses sexual identity openly; develops a public gay political consciousness" (422–23); and "creates a sense of community based
on sexuality" (454). Rofel eloquently articulates the political stakes
of interrogating such a project, stakes that are rendered all the more
acute by the location from which such formulations emanate—the
West, that "imaginary location that can interpret its located concerns
as a world-historical origin point" (455): "The manner in which we
imagine transcultural processes of identification shapes the kind of
alliances we create—or fail to create—to address the protean forms of
homophobia around the world and, in related fashion, the culturally
specific normalizations imposed through sex" (453).

What Rofel's critique of Altman suggests, in part, is that there are stakes in separating gendered definitions from sexual ones for a particular model of "modern" Western homosexuality, stakes evidently shared by Halperin in his construction of the modern homosexual.[31] These stakes may not, however, be generalizable beyond a relatively restricted time and place, and beyond very specific political, economic, and social formations. The particular distinctions Halperin makes between modern and premodern sexual identity may indeed continue to provoke Sedgwick's concern about creating an illusory consensus of knowingness around the genuinely unknown, specifically with regard to gender. They risk suggesting that gender — and perhaps also social status — is a largely superseded category in modernity's conception of sexual identity and that it is not crucial to the construction of sexual subjectivity. One point to make might be that, for women at least, then and now, gender and sexuality are inextricable and coextensively constituted. Halperin's later essay, by invoking the history of male homosexuality, seems to have registered this objection, though the book retracts the specificity of the gendered title. But this definitional restriction does not solve the political problems attendant upon the argument. To suggest that gender may no longer figure prominently in modernity's constructions of sexual subjectivity, while not, I assume, the intent of the distinctions Halperin draws, carries with it consequential political effects on the level of analysis as well as organizing. It may, at least potentially, present obstacles to understanding the particular struggles of queer sexual communities that centrally concern gender, such as movements for intersex, transgender, and transsexual rights and recognition. What is at stake, then, in Halperin's taxonomic project — even more prominently articulated in "How to Do the History of Male Homosexuality" than in "Forgetting Foucault" — of disassembling relations between gender (the old regime of sexual subjectivity) and sexuality (the new) for the "modern" homosexual man?[32]

Sexual Subjectivity and the Literary Text

Foucault's history of sexuality privileges texts that more readily yield institutional discourse — law codes, theological tracts, and medical texts, for example. This fact both helps to determine the kind of discursive constructions that emerge in the premodern and the modern and passes over questions about sexual subjectivity of the sort Halperin raises in his reading of two intertextually related short stories, one by Apuleius (from *The Golden Ass*) and the other a "rewrite" of the same story in Boccaccio's *Decameron*.[33] To raise the question of sexual subjectivity rather than identity is to approach the domain of the psychic, if not the psychoanalytic, and to ask questions about desire and identification as elements of subjectivization.[34] Although Halperin stresses that the point he wishes to make "is a historical one, not a literary one" (38/105), it is probably no accident that the textual evidence marshaled for such a discussion is "literary," or "fictional," and thus thoroughly immersed in the domain of the (not necessarily normatively) subjective. His wish to make an exclusively historical point out of fictional material might even be seen as a symptom of a desire to contain interpretation for the sake of theoretical generalization. Thus, too, Foucault may not have used much fiction, because it could not be easily generalized into the theoretico-historical sweep of the argument. But it was also precisely institutionalized — and normative — discourses that Foucault was interested in, because he had a point to make about the discursive apparatuses of the state and their dispersion in modernity and thus about the productive powers of normative discourse and the discourses of normativity.[35]

It would be interesting to ask whether the availability of certain documents and not others from premodernity produces the impression that the primary discourses governing sexuality were legal and religious. The survival of apparatuses of punishment and their use by historians as the primary sources of information on sexuality condition our knowledge of dominant discursive constructions of sex, just as the availability to scrutiny of medical, psychiatric, and pedagogical discourses in modernity allows for the hypothesis that sex is constituted as a problem of truth. Would a different picture concerning premodernity have emerged, for example, were literary texts from the period also scrutinized for their constructions and deployments of sex? Halperin seems to suggest just such a conclusion in his discussion of Boccaccio.

Following Jonathan Walters's study of these two texts, Halperin deploys intertextual comparisons that permit one to identify historically determined ideological specificities, or ideologemes, by examining the departures of the later text from the earlier one in order to make a point about the "evolution" of a certain mode of sexual subjectivity.[36] The story is about a husband who returns home early to discover a young man, with whom his wife has been having an affair, concealed in his house. In both versions, Apuleius's and Boccaccio's, the husband appears unperturbed by the discovery and volunteers to share the wealth, so to speak. But in *The Golden Ass* the husband takes the youth to bed and then has him beaten; as Walters points out, "the husband's having sex with the young man is described as an assault on an unwilling partner, an extra-legal punishment, justified revenge for the 'damage to his honour.'"[37] In the *Decameron*, the narrator of the tale comments, "Dopo la cena, quello che Pietro si divisasse a sodisfacimento di tutti e tre, m'è uscito di mente; so io ben cotanto, che la mattina vegnente infino in su la Piazza fu il giovane, non assai certo qual più stato si fosse la notte o moglie o marito, accompagnato" (117; "After supper, what Pietro devised for the satisfaction of all three has escaped my mind; but this much I know, that on the following morning the youth was escorted back to the public square not altogether certain which he had the more been that night, wife or husband" [441]). Violence is neither explicit nor necessarily implied, and the moral of the story bawdily encourages women in their infidelities.[38] As Walters demonstrates, in Apuleius, the husband's sexual act with the boy signifies little regarding the orientation of his sexuality; rather it is mostly an indication of his status and age/gender dominance.[39] The sex act is a punishment, an assertion of dominance by the man over the boy: "Solus ipse cum puero cubans gratissima corruptarum nuptiarum vindicata perfruebatur" (178; "[he] lay alone with the boy and enjoyed the most gratifying revenge for his ruined marriage" [179]).[40] In Boccaccio, however, the sex act with the boy signals instead Pietro di Vinciolo's sexual preference for boys over women (his preferences are explicitly referred to in the tale). Walters's reading—and Halperin's too—thus argue that whereas in Apuleius it is not a matter of marking the deviance of the subject of desire, in Boccaccio the story depends on an understanding of Pietro's proclivities as deviant and thus not "normal."[41]

For Walters, the Apuleian tale illustrates the degree to which ancient Greek and Roman masculinity is a matter of gender, not sex. What he finds in Boccaccio, on the contrary, is an illustration of "one of the earliest portrayals in Western culture of a man defined by his sexuality, which is somehow his most deeply defining characteristic, and which tells 'the truth' about him" (27). Halperin will agree up to a point but argues that Pietro's deviant subjectivity falls short of the definition of modern homosexuality: "Pietro's inclination is not the same thing as a sexual orientation, much less a sexual identity or form of life, to be sure: for one thing, his sexual preference seems contained, compartmentalized, and does not appear to connect to any other feature of his character, such as a sensibility, a set of personal mannerisms, a style of gender presentation, or a psychology" (41/107).[42]

The point of Walters's study of the intertextual and ideologically significant relation between Apuleius and Boccaccio, and its relevance for the history of homosexuality, is to encourage us to examine "our" "modern" notions of gender as they may or may not apply to the ancient Greek and Roman world. Walters performs a similar "we know whereof we speak" in relation to the meaning of modern gender to the one Halperin performs in relation to modern homosexuality (and, indeed, to gender as well), but Walters's questions carry some radical implications, including the necessity of asking whether the modern category "women" is ultimately a meaningful one for the ancient world (31). For him, Greek and Roman gender separates adult men from "unmen" or "not fully men," categories that could be said to include youths, slaves, eunuchs, sexually passive males, and women (30–31).[43] Thus he demonstrates that gender itself is a far more complex notion than we might at first assume. He cites L. P. Hartley's phrase to underscore his point: " 'The past is a foreign country: they do things differently there' " (31), though his conclusion also suggests that a reexamination of the past's categories of sexuality and gender might, in turn, introduce some "otherness" into our own.[44] What might it mean, then, to bring into "our" modern, Western discussions of homosexual identity and sexual subjectivity the "otherness" of gender that Halperin consigns to an earlier era of the "historical evolution" of (male) homosexuality?[45]

In Boccaccio's text, subjectivity is a more vexed problem than Halperin's observations allow: it is inextricably bound up with both sexuality and gender as well as with the question of "historical" and "literary" reading. Halperin's argument about Pietro's nonnormativity assumes, for example, not only that sodomy was proscribed and punished by law but also that Boccaccio's society was homophobic, categorizing an adult male's sexual desire for a boy as deviance. He supports this by referring to the narratorial judgment articulated in the text (which he sometimes equates with Boccaccio): "What Boccaccio marks specifically as deviant about Pietro, . . . is his desire."[46] Perhaps, then, Halperin's assumption applies not mainly to the historical context but specifically to Boccaccio—or, should one wish to be more "literarily" specific, Dioneo, the narrator—who in this case would be an anxious homophobe enlisting readers in his playful derision of Pietro the sodomite.

These questions about historical context, narrative perspective, and authorial subjectivity in turn give rise to others: the story takes place in Perugia; since Boccaccio was a Florentine, might we read the peculiarities of the townspeople's low opinion of Pietro as a comment on the rigid heteronormative morality of Perugini in contrast to Florentines? Guido Ruggiero notes that a striking number of Venetian sodomy trials involved or invoked Florentines, while according to Manlio Stocchi, early modern Italian references to being in Perugia or being a Perugino were a way of insinuating the homosexual or sodomitic character of the person described and thus that the line "Fu in Perugia" that signals the beginning of the story also signals its sodomitic thematics.[47] Pietro comes from a prominent Perugian family and is somewhat derisively designated as "rich" (*ricco*); is Boccaccio therefore ascribing to him a general sort of decadence and deceitfulness attributable to the nobility?[48] The narrative itself, it turns out, elaborates upon the question of sodomy and its punishment throughout: as both Stocchi and Susan Gaylard indicate, Ercolano's wife's lover is discovered because he sneezes from breathing sulphurous fumes (112; V.10.35), while Pietro, denouncing his wife's hypocrisy, makes a similar reference to Sodom and Gomorrah when he wishes that " 'venir possa fuoco da cielo che tutte v'arda' " (115; V.10.54; " 'fire might come from heaven to burn you all up' " [440]).[49] The wife, though provided here with the ideal opportunity for a rejoinder, equivocates instead: " 'Io ne son molto certa che tu vorresti che fuoco venisse da cielo che tutte ci ardesse, . . . ma alla croce di Dio egli non ti verrà fatto' " (115; V.10.55–56; " 'Of this much, indeed, I am mighty well assured, that you would have fire come from heaven to burn us women all up, . . . but, by Christ His Cross, you shall not get your wish'" [440]); as Gaylard notes, "the wife's phrase . . . '*non ti verrà fatto*' can be read in context as meaning that the punishment will not be done *for* the husband, but could also mean that the punishment will not be done *to* him" (40). The dialogic exchange between husband and wife is a political and ethical one marked by the (deadly serious) play on the Biblical—but also literal—punishment for sodomy: to be burned at the stake. In other words, does Pietro's sexual preference and his dislike of women justify his wife's adultery, on the one hand, or, on the other, is the wife's hypocrisy equal to (or perhaps, as Gaylard suggests, worse than) her husband's "sin"? Such a reading, both historical and literary, renders potentially problematic the attempt to locate a normative perspective in the text.

Further, in the *Decameron*, the embeddedness of each story in a series of frames designed in part to highlight the perspectival nature of the articulated subjectivities of the text—individual storytellers telling stories and an "I" narrator that identifies itself in the preface and the epilogue of the work—increases the difficulty of identifying normative discourse. From the outset, readers are presented with contradictory and conflicting narratorial discourses, compounded by the fact that each tale is attributed to a particular speaker within the fiction of the frame. In the preface, the Boccaccio-narrator comes out as a heterosexual who, having been rejected by his lady, suffered from severe melancholy and, because he remembers the pain of having been in love, endeavors to write a book that will offer succor to ladies who are secretly in love and thus in danger of similar suffering. The book will both entertain them and provide them with useful advice. He also calls the work a *Galeotto*, invoking the book that served as seditious go-between for Dante's Paolo and Francesca and caused them to commit adultery, the sexual perversion and crime punishable by law in early modern Italy that is suggestively invoked in V.10 as potentially corresponding to the crime of sodomy. One aspect of this narrative subjectivity to note is that it both identifies with and desires "the ladies." Thus, we might also ask of the narratorial intent of the tenth story of the fifth day whether it is specifically directed at and focalized through the (heterosexual) wife, a "giovane compressa, di pelo rosso e accesa" (107; "thickset, red-haired, hot-complexioned wench" [434]) (the name of the Boccaccio-narrator/persona's lover is Fiammetta, or little flame, which may be hinted at in the reference to the young woman's red skin or hair). This might also explain why Pietro's subjectivity is construed as deviant, since from the wife's perspective his choice to marry her when he does not desire women is absurd and gratuitously perverse.[50] In Boccaccio's story, as Walters also remarks, the narrator's sympathies often seem to be with the adulterous wife, whereas in Apuleius they are clearly with the husband.

The narrator's simultaneous identification with and desire for the ladies might also be seen to signal a deviant—or at least explicitly perverse—narratorial subjectivity, marked in the text by the reference to deviation itself, the *Galeotto*, which turned souls away from the proper path and toward sexual sin. The copresence of identification and desire in a member of one gender for a member of the gender that is deemed to be its opposite in heteronormative modernity in the West is, in those modern terms, a deviant sexual and gendered subjectivity, even if—or rather, perhaps, because—it is widely associated with the subjectivity adopted by early modern male European writers of secular poetry and prose (being a writer of fiction, if you are a man, is not a normatively masculine occupation, and Boccaccio was a cleric as well).[51] Thus it would seem that if we assume an identity between the Boccaccio-narrator and Dioneo, we are still unable to ascribe to the narratorial condemnatory position in the tale the status of normativity. On the contrary, the author/narrator here is also queer. None of these readings contradict Halperin's argument that Pietro's subjectivity is a marked one, but the meaning of the marked subjectivity shifts depending on how normativity is being construed and where it is being located in the text.

Fiction may or may not yield normative discourse; the literary text alone is insufficient to decide the question. Literature and its techniques of reading explicitly resist the project of conceptual categorization and classification through the complex rhetorical displacements of subjectivity and the impossibility of closing off—delineating the boundaries of—the field of signification. This would constitute the "resistance to theory" Halperin identifies as profoundly Foucauldian: "*The History of Sexuality, Volume I,* in short, does not contain an original theory of sexuality; if anything, its theoretical originality lies in its refusal of existing theory and its consistent elaboration of a critical anti-theory. It offers a model demonstration of how to dismantle theories of sexuality, how to deprive them of their claims to legitimate authority" (45/110). *Fiction* might also be the name for that discourse able to resist the "dangerous consensus of knowingness" around the question of the normative by reiterating the profound perversities of discursive subjectivity itself.[52]

Conclusion

Halperin returns to broader historical considerations regarding sexuality at the end of his readings. He says that he wants his argument to encourage us to "inquire into the construction of sexual identities before the emergence of sexual orientations, and to do this without recurring [*How to Do the History*: "*without* recurring necessarily"] to modern notions of sexuality." His suggestion that we supplement our definitions of identity with "more refined" concepts of "partial identity, emergent identity, transient identity, semi-identity, incomplete identity, proto-identity, or subidentity" reinstates a notion of historical progression that makes modernity the culmination of identity, even as it attributes to modernity a unitary temporality and conceptual coherence across space/geography. But he says further that his intent is not so much to reinstall identity as a historical category as to "*indicate the multiplicity of possible historical connections between sex and identity*" (43/109; emphasis original).

If Foucault's project in *The History of Sexuality* was in part, as I understand it, to critique modernity's production of a field of truth called sexuality, then I would regard the project Halperin outlines here as distinctively anti-Foucauldian in that it seems to encourage historians of the pre- and early modern not to take up the Foucauldian project of producing a history of sexuality, that is, the history of the production of a particular set of discursive apparatuses around sex as the truth of the subject, but instead to work within those very apparatuses to produce truths about people of the past through sex, to formulate a progressive taxonomic history of same-sex sexual behaviors in their distance from and proximity to a modernity defined by sexual identity or orientation.[53] This is not a critical

genealogy in the Foucauldian sense, at least not insofar as a genealogy may be said to reveal power's implication in the production
of discursive regimes and function to articulate the palimpsestic and
motivated character of modernity's discourses of truth.

Halperin's later essay, in fact, seems to produce an aporetic split
between the two impulses, the Foucauldian and the historical/taxo-
nomic. On the one hand, it concludes with a schematic representation in the form of a chart or table of the five "prehomosexual"
categories of masculine sex/gender identity Halperin has been discussing, while on the other it makes the Foucauldian argument that
"homosexuality is part of a new system of sexuality" and that "homo/
hetero categories function . . . to manage, by differentiating and
disciplining ["them,"] unranked masses of notionally identical 'individuals.' One name for this technique of governing individuals en
masse ["by comparing and differentiating them"] is *normalization*."[54]
If this latter claim holds some validity—and I think it does—what
possible project of liberation is served by "differentiating and disciplining" the past in relation to the present? And if, indeed, "normalization" consists in part of reorganizing gender hierarchies along a
homo/hetero axis, then perhaps we might wish to bring back some
of gender's Old World otherness into our theoretical discussions of
sexual identity and subjectivity. New queer community formations
are already doing so, and in so doing, they are remaking the category
of "gender" in complex and perhaps unforeseeable ways.[55]

In "Don't Ask, Don't Tell: Murderous Plots and Medieval Secrets,"
Lochrie takes up a related part of Sedgwick's argument concerning
the double binds of the "enabling but dangerous incoherence" of
the "self-contradictory discursive fields of force" around minoritizing and universalizing understandings of sexual definition.[56] Lochrie
shows how regimes of secrecy and disclosure function as murderous plots around medieval gender and sexuality on the one hand and
"contemporary structures of oppression attaching to homosexuality,"
such as the closet and the military policy of "don't ask, don't tell,"
on the other (139). Her essay provides a compelling argument for the
coextensive analysis of both gender and sexuality in history, for both
feminism and queer theory, in our discussions of acts and identities in
the past: "Gender and sexuality are both part of secrecy's plot and its
historical span, and if we don't ask or pursue these aspects of the plot

together, we shall merely be protecting ourselves from the reaches of that ideological script and the murderous plots it generates" (149–50). Thus, following Foucault's call for a "history of sexuality," one of the things that scholars of the premodern might contribute to current discussions is precisely an analysis of the interstructuring of gender and sexuality, whose "ideological script" provides telling documentation for a genealogy of modernity's discursive regimes.

4

Queer Nation

EARLY/MODERN FRANCE

In chapter 3 I explored what occlusions might be said to occur in doing the history of homosexuality, and what problems arise not only in relation to historical questions but also insofar as a history proposes itself as singular, definitive, and about a predefined category. I also wanted to demonstrate some of the destabilizing and antinormative effects on historical thinking produced by texts that flaunt their status as fictional, imaginative, or literary. What if, instead, we think of a literary text intervening into historical representation in an effort to comment on what Jonathan Goldberg calls the "logic of historicity," which is itself also a textual logic?[1] In my efforts to think through how a fantasmatic historiography might proceed, I engage in the archeological project of reconstructing an ideology from the body of official discourses on family and sovereignty in sixteenth-century France and reading a fictional text as an imagined response to that ideology. This chapter also performs a critical genealogy of state discourses on "woman," marriage, and the family but, rather than finding a shift away from statist management strategies for bodies and populations, I chart instead the transhistorical continuities between early modern techniques of social management and current discursive productions of the state's investment in social regimes of bodily difference.

Following Foucault, feminist scholars, critical race-studies scholars, and historians of sexuality have argued that the modern European nation-state manages its population through the proliferative discursive production of differentially categorized human bodies.[2] Such discursive production is seen to be dispersed in a way that includes and extends Althusser's notion of ideological state apparatuses to disciplines such as medicine, psychiatry, and education.[3] In Foucault's argument, the genealogy of this process importantly charts a shift away from the state's legislative prohibition, toward typological specification and description and thus toward greater indirection and local, contingent deployments of power-knowledge.[4] While this historical account helps to clarify aspects of the dispersal of state power in modernity, it also potentially obscures what continuities there may be between premodern juridical formations in the nascent state and modern efforts to manage bodies through forms of identifiable state power. My argument unfolds within what might at first glance appear to be an older historical and theoretical framework, examining the way the state and "classes" of people collude in the production and management of human bodies across time. This is not intended to minimize historical differences between pre- or early modernity and modernity, but rather to highlight the persistence, over time, of the state in gender, race, and sexual formations, and to provide a critical genealogy for some of the resistances of human agents to the state's efforts at social management and control.

I am interested—as part of a pre- or early modern genealogy of the relation between the nation-state, nationalism, and its human subjects—in the ways gender, "race," and sexuality interrelate in early statist attempts to fashion the nation. In many analyses of feminism's histories—as in Foucault's accounts of the emergence of counter-discursive movements or "reverse discourse" aggregated around the claim of identity (101)—the modern nation-state plays an important role in precipitating feminism as a critique and a political and social movement.[5] My focus on a sixteenth-century literary text by a woman highly placed in the French monarchy suggests a long trajectory for the counterdiscourse that might be called feminism, and it also points to ways in which, very early on in Western Europe's nationalist histories, nation, gender, sexuality, and race are intertwined—queerly so—both from the point of view of the state and in the utopian counterorders imagined to intervene in its workings. Further, early modern French nationalism demonstrates that not only are gender and "race" (or blood) at stake in the construction of the nation-state from its inception, but so too is heteronormativity. The coarticulation of these elements in the production of national subjects may also help to explain why feminist responses, when they have targeted gender or women alone, work to shore up, rather than dismantle, the exclusionary imperatives of the nation.

The 1999 Pacte Civil de Solidarité (PACS), which created a new section in the French civil code and established national domestic partner legislation, brought into sharp relief once again the French state's continuing investment in legally defining and configuring kinship arrangements. Michael Lucey has linked this moment to the earlier Napoleonic Civil Code's efforts to legislate and thus also regulate the hegemonic normative family form, especially in relation to the inheritance of property.[6] PACS, which permits people of the same sex to be legally declared partners, nevertheless retains much of the Napoleonic code's definition of who counts as an heir. In other words, a domestic partner does not benefit from the category of "spouse" for the purposes of inheritance, among other things, thus demonstrating not only the patently juridical definition of "family" in the French civil code but also its heteronormative intent.[7] As Lucey notes of the domestic partnership debates triggered by PACS, "talk about nature and sexual difference . . . is in fact little more than an alibi for a discussion and for legislation that is much more centrally about property rights and inheritance practices, as well as sexual oppression" (16). Here he echoes anthropologist John Borneman's remark that "marriage, gender, and the symbolics of blood, then, enter into social relations not as prior to sexuality but as part of a matrix of power relations."[8] Lucey's work thus contributes to a critical history of the relation between the state and heteronormativity and their coimplication in the property relations that, since Engels, have been thought to originate or be reflected in patriarchal family forms.[9]

Taking my cue from Lucey's work, I want to argue that another crucial moment in the genealogy of the French state's investment in kinship arrangements occurs earlier, in the sixteenth century, the period to which is normally attributed an initial consolidation of the French nation as a state, with elements resembling the modern form of the nation-state, such as a distinct political and bureaucratic apparatus, centralized taxation methods, legal reforms, a juridico-legal system, and a parliament. For this period it is difficult to name the state on the one hand and kinship on the other, since state politics are very deeply and indistinguishably a matter of family relations, given that sovereignty is a legal, metaphysical, and blood concept that binds together state, God, and family. Thus it would in some respects be anachronistic to refer to these two spheres, state and family, as though distinctions of public and private, political and social (or civil), governed their relations.[10] As Sarah Hanley notes, "Early modern monarchies were characterized politically by intertwined private-public (family-state) relations."[11]

Marriage served as one of the primary state-making instruments. On the one hand, the control of marital arrangements meant the control of property and its transmission through inheritance; on the other, marriage (and bio-legal reproduction) was the primary means by which sovereignty (and the sovereign) achieved self-replication. Marriage was thus, unsurprisingly, a focus of contestation in the early modern nation-state, in part because it was a peculiar arrangement, subject to both canon and civil law, and thus the site of a convergence of potentially conflicting interests between church and state but also among people.

As in the case of the monarchy, the ruling class's interest in marriage involved inheritance: in the sixteenth century there emerged, through the system of venality—whereby political positions became inheritable goods and could also, therefore, be bought and sold—a class of professional lawyers, the *noblesse de robe*, who staffed administrative and judicial offices in the kingdom. A system was therefore instituted whereby political offices could be hereditarily transmitted to the next generation as family property. This particular interweaving of family and state interests created an incentive—realized over the course of the sixteenth century in France—to increase the power of constitutional and civil law over that of ecclesiastical or canon law and to bring marriage, the key to state making as well as to the hereditary transmission of property and goods, under the control of secular law and thus of family and state.

Meanwhile, from Gratian's twelfth-century *Concordia discordantium canonum*, which summarized case law and opinion, until the mid-sixteenth century in France, consent of the parties involved was the sine qua non of a legal marriage, which came under the jurisdiction of canon law and the ecclesiastical courts. Gratian's *Decretum* tellingly asks the question, "May a daughter be given in marriage against her will?" and answers it with reference to paternal authority: "A father's oath cannot compel a girl to marry one to whom she has not as-sented."[12] Until the sixteenth century, it was also theoretically pos-sible for people to marry without the consent of their families, an event referred to as "clandestine marriage" and repeatedly targeted for regulation throughout the century. The Parlement of Paris in 1556 promulgated an edict against clandestine marriages, and in 1557, the king, Henri II, also issued an edict against them, which was to be the subject of a treatise by Jean Coras, the man who would later be one of the judges in the trial of Martin Guerre (also a story about clandes-tine marriage).[13] Natalie Zemon Davis argues that until 1564, when the last session of the Council of Trent established specific guide-lines to ascertain the validity of a marriage, consent of the partners alone continued to constitute a valid union even in the absence of a priest and witnesses. "People," she argues, "used [clandestine mar-riage] for reasons of their own: they were minors and their parents were opposed to the marriage; they were marrying within a prohib-ited degree of kinship and could not get a dispensation; they wanted to have intercourse and this was the only way to do it; one of the partners was already married to a person in another place."[14] In prac-tice, of course, families exercised the maximum control possible in contracting alliances and thus, over the course of the Middle Ages, "a contest developed between two institutions [family and church] for control over the connubial fate of children."[15]

Another factor that may have shaped the state's and monarch's in-terest in marriage was the fact that, in the early 1500s, legists and scholars schooled in the humanist techniques of philology and his-torical research proved the fraudulence of the French Salic Law, which was supposed to exclude women from succession to monar-chic office in the kingdom. As a result, the exclusion of women from rule was no longer a constitutional matter.[16] Elsewhere in Europe queens ruled; further, in sixteenth-century France, foreign brides for kings were the rule rather than the exception. Some of them— most notoriously Catherine de Medici—were installed as queen re-gents, while kings regularly failed to generate successors: only two of the five Valois kings, for example, had legal marital progeny. Thus, argues Hanley, legists and members of the parliaments developed a French law canon "which secured legal foundations for the male right to govern along the lines of a Marital Regime in law."[17] This law canon—defined as the articulation, compilation, and deployment of public law (patterns of laws and case precedents condensed into a series of political maxims) and as the production of political rituals—also gave shape to the French nation as a state, for it provided an "indigenous French body of laws . . . able to contend with the law codes cited . . . by other European states and the papacy" (109).

Over the course of the sixteenth century, then, these legists and members of the parliaments developed a body of laws—what Hanley characterizes as a Marital Regime government—which secured secular legal foundations for a male right to govern and to transmit property and which definitively excluded women from the political sphere. This French legal canon encompassed public law (which addressed the constitutional foundations of the state encapsulated in the marital maxim "The king is the husband and political spouse of the kingdom"); civil law (which governed the family and marriage); and natural law (which established the natural superiority of males over females and the priority of male seminal transmission in matters of succession). Thus the king was the husband of the kingdom; the inalienable dowry brought to him from the kingdom was his territory; and his royal sons were the political progeny born to him of this union: "They are children of the French people and the kingdom." This interweaving of political and marital relations produced an intimate linkage between "family formation and state building by contractually uniting king and kingdom in a political state marriage likened legally to that of husband and wife in a social civil marriage."[18] Finally, natural law also worked to ensure that the king alone could produce heirs to the throne: the coupling of king and kingdom amounted to an "autogenetic male generative act" (111). Based in arguments from Aristotelian reproductive science that male seed was formative while the female contributed only matter, political theorists developed a biogenetic seminal theory of authority, whereby husbands produce heirs and kings produce successors through seminal creation. Even though, as Lorraine Daston and Katherine Park have argued, there were at the time competing scientific theories of reproduction, notably from Galen, this is the one that seems to have predominated as a political maxim in part no doubt to prevent succession to the crown from unions involving French queens and foreign husbands.[19] It also effectively excluded women from rule, since only men born of the seed of kings could inherit the throne. This theory finds its culmination in the shift in monarchic public policy in the 1570s regarding the principles of succession from a policy that designated Peers of France (the king and his barons) to one that specified Princes of the Blood (direct descendants of the king and his cadet lines).[20] Blood and semen here are also used interchangeably, further demonstrating the tacit coarticulation of racial and sexual theories and policies in early modern French nation-state formation: at one and the same time, French nationhood is defined as male and not foreign, the familiar configuration associated with nationalism here articulated as a set of concrete and discrete elements of political theory and social practice.[21] Thus, this Marital Regime government is also a strategy that accomplishes the distinction between France and its outside.

Begetting royal sons on the kingdom is either a surprisingly generative form of onanism or else a kind of masculine sodomitic relation that bears fruit.[22] This autogenetic fantasy, an early misogynistic and xenophobic defense mechanism of the state's formation, thus reveals itself to be strangely queer. While we understand the future of this formation as a certain nationalist ruling-class homosociality, it is interesting to find its ideological building blocks so materially fashioned as to denormativize nation and homosociality and betray the queerness Eve Kosofsky Sedgwick locates there.[23] Further, it illustrates one of the ways in which normativity harbors queerness within it as its foreclosed and forcibly excluded exterior, an interior that, exteriorized, discloses itself in this case in the categories of "women" and "foreigners" as the abjected others of the nation/family. Thus, this formulation of the nation/family can be said to produce both women and foreigners as its constitutive outside.

I want to turn to a story in Marguerite de Navarre's *Heptameron* that may be seen to allegorize the peculiar queerness at work in this fantasy of nation building and that—by strategically deploying the monstrous and feared figure of gynocracy—exposes as incestuous and endogamous sixteenth-century monarchic strategy even as it aspires to a similarly parthenogenetic fantasy of maternal/matriarchal rule. In exposing that patriarchal strategy, while nevertheless substituting for it an equally autocratic maternal one, Marguerite de Navarre's text also reaffirms a racial homogeneity for the state and ultimately endorses its heteronormativity even as it repudiates phallocracy.

I have argued elsewhere that Marguerite de Navarre's *Heptameron* is a social text, an act of indirect intervention into matters of state via the conceit of both "fiction" and "véritable histoire," or "true history."[24] Margaret Ferguson notes that, like Castiglione, who also "rewrites" Boccaccio and stages a battle of the sexes conducted by discussants in a *locus amoenus*, Marguerite de Navarre "gives us the portrait of the author as courtier—someone who needs exquisite skills of persuasion as she attempts to play one of the most difficult of the roles Castiglione's male interlocutors discuss: the role of the courtier not only as 'ornament,' but as educator of the prince."[25] Queen Marguerite de Navarre, sister to King François I, was involved in an international diplomatic tug of war between her brother and her husband (Henri de Navarre) over the marriage of her daughter, Jeanne. The archives reveal her caught between kin (her brother the king) and lineage (her husband), ultimately acting as the obedient subject who imposes the king's will upon both her husband and her daughter. Jeanne—best known historically as a Protestant leader and the mother of the future king Henri IV—seems to have protested her mother's and the king's choice of the husband she eventually married, a marriage that was later annulled on the grounds of nonconsent. Marguerite's fiction at several points articulates a female subject's protests before a female monarch specifically on the issue of consent in the choice of a marriage partner. In her fiction, then, Marguerite de Navarre seems to confront the question of the daughter's agency and "resolve" the conflict of wills in the best interests of both the queen and her subject. Thus Marguerite demonstrates, both textually and in the documented archives of her "life," an active investment in questions of family-state rule and the place of the (sovereign) woman within them, reinvesting the maternal sovereign, in her fiction, with the authority to fashion the state.[26]

Thus, for example, in story 42, Parlamente (the explicitly politically referenced presumed author figure) recounts a pedagogical tale involving a young prince ("'celluy des plus heureux princes de la chrestienté'"; "'the happiest and most fortunate prince in Christendom'"), whose advances are repeatedly refused by an exemplarily virtuous but poor young woman felicitously named Françoise.[27] Unlike so many of the plots of the *Heptameron*'s novellas, where the woman in question would have been taken by force, this story results in the prince's being educated into virtuous and chaste conduct by his namesake (François/Françoise) and, it is suggested, his nation ("françoise") through the figure of a young woman. As if to underline the national allegory at work in the tale, Oisille (one of the storytellers and the spiritual mother of the group) suggests that Françoise would have more aptly served as founding exemplar of virtue than Lucretia, the Roman heroine whose rape and suicide precipitates the Roman republic: "Je ne voy que ung mal, dist Oisille: que les actes vertueux de ceste fille n'ont esté du temps des historiens, car ceulx qui ont tant loué leur Lucresse l'eussent laissé au bout de la plume, pour escripre bien au long les vertuz de ceste-cy" (294); " 'There is only one thing I would regret,' said Oisille, 'and that is that the virtuous actions of this young girl didn't take place in the time of the great [Roman] historians. The writers who praised Lucretia so much would have left her story aside, so that they could describe at length the virtue of the heroine of your story' " (389). Here a certain French nationalism (as against Roman exemplarity) articulates itself, while the feminized figure of France educates its monarch into virtuous conduct, thus becoming herself a historical actor in the development of the French nation-state. In this particular tale, then, fiction and "verité" collude in the production of an indirect intervention in matters of state rule: the fashioning of its sovereign as a chaste and virtuous prince.[28]

Story 30 is about a very young and wealthy widow with a son, who decides not to remarry, "tant pour le regret qu'elle avoit de son mary que pour l'amour de son enfant" (229; "whether out of sorrow at the loss of her husband or whether out of her love for her child" [317]).[29] Thus already there appears the double bind that Christiane Klapisch-Zuber has named "the cruel mother" syndrome: on the one hand, it is a young widow's duty (to her family of birth) to remarry and thus to place her wealth back into circulation; on the other, it is a sign of her devotion to her family of marriage that she does not, retaining the wealth for the male heir of that family (her son).[30] The delicate and sometimes aporetic positioning between kin and marriage (or lineage), between endogamy and exogamy, both crucially defines woman as currency and gift and specifically brings the particular dif-

ficulties of Marguerite's position between these two lines into relief. In Marguerite's case, of course, loyalty to the family of birth is
also loyalty to the king of France. Thus positioned on that line that
Claude Lévi-Strauss argues demarcates civilization from its outside
(what he sometimes calls "nature"), the widow decides to withdraw
from the social order altogether.[31] Klapisch-Zuber, it is interesting
to note, remarks that when women in early modern Italy chose to
remain within the family of marriage — thus ensuring the financial
solvency of their husband's heirs — they were said to become both a
father and a mother to their dead husband's children (128).

 The widow finds a holy man to serve as the son's "maistre d'escolle"
(schoolmaster or tutor), while she herself has a "damoiselle," a young
lady who sleeps in her room. At fourteen, when the son reaches
puberty, he begins to pursue the lady-in-waiting, at which point
she complains to her mistress. The widow does not believe her but
hatches a plan to trade places with the damoiselle and wait to see if
the young man goes to her bed. If he does, she decides she will "chas-
tier si bien son filz, qu'il ne coucheroit jamais avecq femme qu'il ne
luy en souvynt" (230; "give her son such a chastising that he would
never in the whole of his life get in bed with a woman without re-
membering it" [318]). One wonders at this point whether the maternal intention is not already to produce an incestuous mother/son
relation, given that the goal is for the son to think about his mother
whenever he has sex with a woman.[32] He does, of course, make his
way to the damoiselle's room, and the mother, incredulous, waits so
long with him in the bed that "elle convertit sa collere en ung plaisir
trop abominable, obliant le nom de mere" (230; "her anger turned to
pleasure, a pleasure so abominable, that she forgot she was a mother"
[318]). She becomes pregnant; the narrator remarks, "en ceste nuict
là, engrossa de celluy, lequel elle vouloit garder d'engrossir les autres"
(231; "that night she became pregnant by the very one whom she desired to prevent getting others with child" [318]). She then sends her
son off to war to hide her shame and gets her brother to collude in
the concealment of the birth of a beautiful daughter, who is immediately sent out to wet nurse and to live with a faraway relative. The
son, back from the wars in Italy, begs his mother to permit him to
return home, whereupon she refuses to see him until he has married
a woman he loves very much.

The son meets and marries the widow's daughter, his daughter and sister, much to the mother's horror and dismay. She consults with the theologians as to what course of action to take, whereupon they advise the following: "que la dame ne debvoit jamais rien dire de ceste affaire à ses enffans, car, quant à eulx, veu l'ignorance, ilz n'avoient point peché, mais qu'elle en debvoit toute sa vie faire penitence, sans leur en faire ung seul semblant" (233; "that the lady should never say anything to her children, for they had acted in ignorance and consequently had not sinned. But she, their mother, was to do penance for the rest of her life without giving the slightest indication of it to them" [321]).

The two live extraordinarily happily ever after; they "s'entre-aymoient si fort que jamais mary ny femme n'eurent plus d'amitié et semblance, car elle estoit sa fille, sa seur et sa femme, et luy à elle, son pere, frere et mary" (233; "Never was there such love between husband and wife, never were a husband and wife so close. For she was his daughter, his sister, his wife. And he was her father, brother, and husband" [321]).[33] Not only, then, do they desire each other, but they also accomplish that "grande amitié" or friendship that Marguerite's Platonic theory of conjugal reciprocity holds up as the highest ideal of the marriage relation. The mother devotes the rest of her life to doing penance. One editor of an early edition of the *Heptameron* includes in his notes epitaphs found in churches that pose the riddle of kin relations in this fashion: "Here lies the child, the parent, the sister, the brother, the wife and the husband, but there are only two people here" or again, "Here lies the son, here lies the mother, here lies the daughter with the father, here lies the sister, here lies the brother, here lie the wife and the husband, but there are only three bodies here." The editor also includes contemporary compilations of the Oedipus and Jocasta story.[34]

But the differences between this tale and *Oedipus* are striking: first of all, this is not a tragedy. No one dies. The young couple's love is confirmed, their marriage intact; indeed, they are the perfect couple. Second, the perspective of the tale is the mother's rather than the son's or father's. Thus, while the tragedy of Oedipus chronicles the destruction of the polis through endogamous kinship relations, and others as monstrous the maternal figure, this tale affirms as utterly harmonious the "friendship" and "resemblance" of the product of incestuous unions. In order for this to be achieved, the mother must, of course, be condemned and excluded from the reproductive cycle she sets in motion, which was what she had originally been planning for herself all along. Nevertheless, she remains—autogenetically and parthenogenetically, as it were—the source and origin of a bloodline.

This fantasy of maternal sovereignty—one that I have analyzed elsewhere in Marguerite's text—may well constitute a perverse intervention into matters of state-making in early modern France, a commentary on masculine and sovereign autogenetic theory.[35] Lévi-Strauss's remark about this aspect of incest, a social incest which, for him, includes marriage, is telling: "L'inceste, entendu au sens le plus large, consiste à obtenir par soi-même, et pour soi-même, au lieu d'obtenir par autrui, et pour autrui" (561; "Incest, in the broadest sense of the word, consists in obtaining by oneself, and for oneself, instead of by another, and for another" [489]).[36] This fantasy also resembles the fantasy, articulated in story 42, of twin sovereign subjects of the nation distinguished only by the masculine and feminine forms of the proper name (of the nation): François and Françoise.

Also unlike *Oedipus*, the incest in this story is doubled: mother with son and daughter/sister with father/brother. The result is that every kinship position in the family has its heterosexual desirous counterpart. In the beginning of the story, the mother and son each have a same-sex double: the son an "homme de saincte vie" (a holy man) who serves as his schoolmaster, the mother a damoiselle who sleeps in her room. The story details the son's departure from his tutor and his initiation into heterosexual desire: "Nature, qui est maistre d'escolle bien secret, le trouvant bien nourry et plein d'oisiveté, luy aprint autre leçon que son maistre d'escolle ne faisoit" (230; "Nature, that most secret of teachers, found that this well-grown lad had nothing to occupy him and began to teach him lessons somewhat different from those of his tutor" [317]); it also details the mother's substitution of her person for the person of the damoiselle. Thus Gayle Rubin's suggestion that prior to or simultaneous with the incest taboo there must also be a taboo on homosexual desire finds a figure here in the movement from a homosocial (perhaps homoerotic) space to the place where sexual difference sets the incest in motion.[37] Could we not say, then, that the fantasy of autogenesis here works as compensatory for the loss occasioned by the necessity of exogamic—or heterosexual—exchange, an exchange that, Lévi-Strauss argues, is necessary to the movement from family to group, or family to society, and, finally, family to nation? Thus even as the text reaffirms its commitment to heterosexuality—however nonnormative that heterosexuality may be—it also renders legible the traces of another order that is left in its wake.

Judith Butler has argued that the melancholia of the subject in heteronormativity is the result of a loss at the origin of subject formation, a loss that is foreclosed, refused as loss, a loss she names as the same-sex object of love. The normative response to this loss, in her rewriting of Freud's theory of sexed subjectivity, is to identify with the same-sex object of love, to incorporate it, and thus to become gendered and heterosexually desiring.[38] In this text, then, the fantasy of incest would be a way of partially preserving the lost object of love as an object of desire, for the marital union of brother/father and daughter/sister produces perfect friendship and perfect "semblance," desire and identification seamlessly joined. This is the "dream" that Lévi-Strauss identifies as "saisir et . . . fixer cet instant fugitif où il fut permis de croire qu'on pouvait ruser avec la loi d'échange, gagner sans perdre, jouir sans partager" (569; "seizing and fixing that fleeting moment when it was permissible to believe that the law of exchange could be evaded, that one could gain without losing, enjoy without sharing" [497]). And indeed, this is also the dream of the widow, whose refusal to reenter an economy of exchange (to remarry) amounts to just such an evasion of the logics of renunciation and sacrifice required by "the traffic in women." Thus the maternal sovereign produces the beginning of a line of succession that cannot be alienated from her domain.

Marguerite's text thus inscribes the subjectivity absent—as Luce Irigaray has so acerbically noted—from Lévi-Strauss's account of woman as gift in the economy of exogamic kinship.[39] In so doing, it also comments on the fantasy of French nationalism as the foreclosed—simultaneously legislated and refused—homoerotic and incestuous desire to obtain, "by oneself, and for oneself," the sweetness ("la douceur," Lévi-Strauss calls it) "d'un monde où l'on pourrait vivre *entre soi*" (570; "of a world in which one might *keep to oneself*" [497]; emphasis original), a fantasy that inextricably joins race, sex, and gender. It is perhaps the inability to mourn that dream that produces the French nation-state's current reassertions of self-sameness. At the very least, this genealogy reveals the repudiated queerness in the explicitly phallocratic formulation of the state's heteronormative imperatives.

In *The Elementary Structures of Kinship*, Lévi-Strauss summarizes Freud's reading of incest in *Totem and Taboo*: "Les satisfactions symboliques dans lesquelles s'épanche, selon Freud, le regret de l'inceste, ne constituent donc pas la commémoration d'un événement. Elles sont autre chose, et plus que cela: l'expression permanente d'un désir de désordre, ou plutôt de contre-ordre" (563; "Symbolic gratifications in which the incest urge finds its expression, according to Freud, do not therefore commemorate an actual event. They are something else, and more, the permanent expression of a desire for disorder, or rather counter-order [491]).[40] The counterorder that the fantasy of maternal autogenetic creation articulates is precisely the gynocracy railed against in French legists' tracts justifying the exclusion of female rule and succession through the female line; it is, in other words, a will to power articulated in the very terms set forth by the French state. In exposing those terms as incestuous, Marguerite's text thus also exposes—as an incestuous autogenesis unmediated by heterosexual reproduction—the queerness of a fantasy of nation-building based on direct father-to-son seminal transmission. And yet this counterorder nevertheless would also seem to affirm the self-replicating principle upon which the state it criticizes is based, for although "women" are now included in the polis, "foreigners" are not. Indeed, in *Antigone's Claim*, Butler suggests that, in addition to the prohibition on incest, a "miscegenation prohibition" would need to be theorized in Lévi-Strauss's discussion of how "cultures maintain an internal coherence precisely through rules that guarantee their reproduction," or "self-replication," one of the social dimensions of incest that persists through exogamic exchange or marriage.[41]

Butler has argued that another figure of incest—Antigone—allegorizes a crisis of kinship in and as the state; she asks, "What in her [Antigone's] act is fatal for heterosexuality in its normative sense? And to what other ways of organizing sexuality might a consideration of that fatality give rise?"[42] She points out that Antigone "fails to produce heterosexual closure" for the Oedipal drama, seeming rather to "deinstitute heterosexuality by refusing to do what is necessary . . . by refusing to become a mother and wife" and ultimately by choosing the tomb over the bridal chamber (76). Marguerite de Navarre's ambiguous heroine also finds herself entombed, consigned to perpetual silence. Her withdrawal, however, does not bring closure; on the contrary, she sets in motion the possibility of a reproductive lineage. One cannot help but think of Marguerite's other, "archival," sovereign strategy, the one that positioned her daughter to become the mother of a king (Henri IV) and thus a royal line. If, in the history of patriarchal feminine exemplarity (albeit in its negative or destructive form), Antigone represents the Greek version of Roman Lucretia as exemplar, then perhaps in this matriarchal scene, the widow is story 30's version of Françoise, a less shattered feminine heroine, agent and catalyst of the nation.[43]

If story 30, with its thematics of incest, is a response to the state's strategic policy of reproductive homosocial incest—a form of gender endogamy—then it posits a utopian (and thus imaginary) solution to a problem that as yet (in the period) has no means of redress, not because of any historical prematurity with respect to political intervention in state policy, but because, in part, nonmonarchical solutions to the problem are neither imaginable nor, for the royalist Marguerite de Navarre, desirable. Further, for this particular sister of a king, imagining the place of the monarch as feminine requires identification—another possible meaning of incest—rather than substitution or replacement. However, in a retrospective reading from the position of a certain (perhaps) feminist and nation-based modernity, this fantasy of maternal sovereignty—protofeminist and protonationalist in appearance—may have had its practical deployments in at least one instance of female sovereignty. Maureen Quilligan argues that the figure of incest and the "fantasized incestuous genealogies" generated elsewhere by Marguerite de Navarre provided the enabling terms of a form of female authority in the Renaissance, a form of authority that culminated in another figure of incest, one who lived to speak and rule: Elizabeth I, who adopts Marguerite's metaphor of incest in her translation of Marguerite's *Mirror of the Sinful Soul* and uses it as "an action that brings about a most spectacularly scandalous halt in the traffic in women."[44] Married to and mother of her people, Elizabeth, virgin queen and also prince, remetaphorizes the incest whose literality undoes both Antigone and Marguerite's widow, abstracting kinship into the terms of the body politic. One might even argue, as some scholars have done, that Elizabeth reinhabits the terms of autogenetic reproductive fantasies by "bisexing" her body into its natural (female) and political (male) forms, or by asserting the possibility of "lesbian" marriage in the image of the ruler wedded to her (female) state.[45] As Goldberg notes of such strategic maneuverings within the terms of power, "Legal disenfranchisements of women in the period are real. Nevertheless, not even these massive closures are effective everywhere, and within the repressions and exclusions of women are also mechanisms that are productive—sites of resistance or of failure within the system, excesses or lacks. [Joan] Kelly's complex analysis of how courtier and court lady could be substituted for each other suggests the possibilities of instabilities in these regulatory measures," possibilities that Elizabeth clearly exploited.[46] Her nonreproductivity, however, a seemingly necessary condition for this abstraction, points to the place where kinship and the state remain joined, where succession and lineage continue to converge in a politics of family and state.

Elizabeth, in any case, is hardly any more exemplary than Antigone or Marguerite's widow. Her discursive self-production illustrates what would persist as a conundrum of liberal feminist political theory in the modern state and civil society: that "women" may either be corporealized or abstracted sovereign subjects, but they cannot be both simultaneously.[47] Further, the nationalism achieved through metaphorical incest serves to confirm the exclusionary racial endogamy of the nation. Nevertheless, the detachment of kinship from blood that Elizabeth's symbolics of sovereignty performs suggests possible ways that kinship—including the same-sex kinship of domestic partnership and adoption and the kinship of political affiliations—would be opened up, in time, to enabling and "transformative articulation[s]" that do not finally consign their subjects to silence or death.[48]

Part Two

FUTURES

5

Queer Spectrality

You walk through my walls,
like a ghost on TV;
you penetrate me.
—ANI DIFRANCO

✍ This final chapter, which represents half of *Queer/Early/Modern*, works affirmingly through the previous critique to think about futurity. Critique and construction, or the art of crafting a language, an image, a structure, a concept out of the available theoretical models, are, for me, two aspects of the process of working through, which, psychoanalytically speaking, leads circuitously to a different place by treading the familiar, familial, forgotten, forsaken paths of the past. That place, arrived at through repetitions, will, it is hoped, open something up to greater possibility. In plain speech and popular culture, the ghost (like the angel) has come of late, it seems, to stand in and speak for a certain collective longing about the past and the future; likewise, in late modern Western theories of subjectivity and historicity, something ghostly is being conjured to address a way of calling and being called to historical and ethical accountability. Here I try to weave together differing and sometimes disparate aspects of how this spectrality is at work in current thinking and doing, and to shape a discourse about how spectral being and doing open us up to porous, permeable pasts and futures—suffused with affect and its ethical implications—that enable us to mourn and also to hope.

Spectrality is a term used by Jacques Derrida to describe a mode of historical attentiveness that the living might have to what is not

spectrality

present but somehow appears as a figure or a voice, a "non-living present in the living present" that is no longer or not yet with us.[1] Spectrality is, in part, a mode of historicity: it describes the way in which "the time is out of joint"; that is, the way the past or the future presses upon us with a kind of insistence or demand, a demand to which we must somehow respond.[2] "Hauntology" as the practice of attending to the spectral, is then a way of thinking and responding ethically within history, as it is a way of thinking ethics in relation to the project of historiography by acknowledging the force of haunting.[3] I would like here to explore the possibilities of spectrality for the project of a queer historiography, to see how it might describe a more ethical relation to the past and the future than our current models permit.

Among the contrasting models of history against which spectrality may be said to work is a necrological model, which foregrounds the idea of burial. We bury the dead, giving them monumental tombs to "commemorate" them. Michel de Certeau has commented on this aspect of historiography, arguing that the historian posits him- or herself as the subject whose writing replaces, covers over, or displaces the other about whom his or her discourse is being elaborated:

> L'autre est le fantasme de l'historiographie. L'objet qu'elle cherche, qu'elle honore et qu'elle enterre . . . "La seule quête historique du 'sens' demeure en effet celle de L'Autre," mais ce projet, contradictoire, vise à "comprendre" et à cacher avec le "sens" l'altérité de cet étranger, ou, ce qui revient au même, à calmer les morts qui hantent encore le présent et à leur offrir des tombeaux scripturaires.

> The other is the phantasm of historiography, the object that it seeks, honors, and buries . . . "The sole historical quest for 'meaning' remains indeed a quest for the Other," but, however contradictory it may be, this project aims at "understanding" and, through "meaning," at hiding the alterity of this foreigner; or, in what amounts to the same thing, it aims at calming the dead who still haunt the present, and at offering them scriptural tombs.[4]

Here, the others, ghosts of historiography, do indeed haunt the present, but the response to that haunting is a kind of anxious appeasement. Certeau illustrates the mastery involved in the project of historiography and the concomitant entombment that accompanies the gesture. In *Heterologies*, he repeats this and includes a warning that opens the way for spectrality: "These voices—whose disappearance every historian posits, but which he replaces with his writing—'re-bite' [*re-mordent*] the space from which they were excluded; they continue to speak in the text/tomb that erudition erects in their place":[5]

> There is an "uncanniness" about this past that a present occupant has expelled (or thinks it has) in an effort to take its place. The dead haunt the living. The past: it "re-bites" [*il re-mord*] (it is a secret and repeated biting). History is "cannibalistic," and memory becomes the closed arena of conflict between two contradictory operations: forgetting, which is not something passive, a loss, but an action directed against the past; and the mnemic trace, the return of what was forgotten, in other words, an action by a past that is now forced to disguise itself. More generally speaking, any autonomous order is founded upon what it eliminates; it produces a "residue" condemned to be forgotten. But what was excluded re-infiltrates the place of its origin. (3–4)

Certeau suggests that the historian's gesture is a melancholic one, an attempt to entomb within writing the lost other of the past. And, as he also suggests, those who are buried—perhaps buried alive— will return to haunt us. This melancholic model is also a response to trauma—the trauma of historicity—yet it is a response that will not acknowledge the trauma or the loss and seeks instead to hush the voices or to "understand" or master them with meaning and discourse.[6]

Another model, which is a kind of corollary to this one, is more directly colonial, and involves outright mastery or appropriation. This is a model Certeau links to Western practices of knowledge production:

> Une structure propre à la culture occidentale moderne s'indique sans doute en cette historiographie: l'intelligibilité s'instaure dans un rapport à l'autre; elle se déplace (ou "progresse") en modifiant ce dont elle fait son "autre"—le sauvage, le passé, le peuple, le fou, l'enfant, le tiers monde. A travers ces variantes entre elles hétéronomes—ethnologie,

histoire, psychiatrie, pédagogie, etc.—, se déploie une problématique articulant un savoir-dire sur ce que l'autre tait, et garantissant le travail interprétatif d'une science ("humaine"). (*L'écriture de l'histoire*, 9)

A structure belonging to modern Western culture can doubtless be seen in this historiography: intelligibility is established through a relation with the other; it moves (or "progresses") by changing what it makes of its "other"—the Indian, the past, the people, the mad, the child, the Third World. Through these variants that are all heteronomous—ethnology, history, psychiatry, pedagogy, etc.—unfolds a problematic form basing its mastery of expression upon what the other keeps silent, and guaranteeing the interpretive work of a science (a "human" science). (*The Writing of History*, 3)

Both of these models have come under scrutiny within U.S. queer political and historical practices in relation to an emergent category of being in queer movement politics, the transsexual/transgendered person, and the rape and murder of "Brandon Teena," which became an emblem and rallying cry for trans-politics.[7] The traumatic event that goes by the proper name of Brandon Teena—itself marked by a kind of belatedness or *Nachträglichkeit*[8]—is, in a sense, a repetition of the violent effacement of difference, usually racial, that constitutes a primary trauma in the U.S. national imaginary and in the autoconstitution of queer movement.[9] " 'Brandon Teena,' " writes C. Jacob Hale, "has become the primary emblem of transphobic violence, an emblem deployed to exemplify the vulnerability of transgendered people."[10] As such, "he" has become the occasion for a broad range of representation and commentary, from fictionalized literary, journalistic, and filmic accounts to documentaries and critical cultural studies.[11]

Although all movements take up the dead and carry them into battle like a banner, the danger of so doing in relation to queer historiography and activism involves an ethical dimension that queer historians might want to honor. In "Brandon" 's case, there is the problematic appropriation of identity that consigned "him" variously to the annals of lesbian history or the fledgling library of the transsexual movement. In either case, precisely the problem of identity with which "he" was involved and involved "himself"—and which turned out to be lethal—is a problem "solved" by activists and historians' taking up of "his" life in the name of a given — and thus also meaningfully defined — category.

Part of what is at stake in the afterlife of "Brandon Teena" is the way "his" person is made meaningful by regulatory regimes of gender that, at the same time, narrow the space of possibility:

> We do not know which trajectory — or which multiple trajectories that appear inconsistent with each other by our lights — this young murder victim would have followed . . . The living . . . bury any aspects of the embodied self this youth constructed that do not fit their own constructions. In so doing, the living refuse to acknowledge that this person was a border-zone dweller: someone whose embodied self existed in a netherworld constituted by the margins of multiple overlapping identity categories. Perhaps Brandon or Teena — or the same person by another chosen name — would have stayed in the borderlands; perhaps she or he would have sought and found a more solid categorical location and language with which to construct and speak that self. We simply do not know. To do more than speculate about this is to collude with the foreclosure of future self-constructions that was so abruptly enacted by murder.[12]

In Hale's account, the dead one is consumed and entombed within categories that are meant to lay to rest troubling uncertainties and that at the same time foreclose the possibility of a future open to what is not already known. The decision to bury "Brandon Teena" within these discursive definitional tombs seems too consonant with "his" violent effacement through a logic of revelation. While John Lotter and Tom Nissen thought themselves to be revealing and thus uncovering the true nature of this person's sex (even as they literally uncovered the nakedness of the body), those who consign "him" to distinct categories of being seem to cover over the ghostly, mobile subjectivity that continues to insist beyond those categories. The destruction brought to bear upon this body revisits a rhetorical trope — what Barbara Spackman calls "the hermeneutic figure *par excellence*" of "the enchantress-turned-hag" — brutally literalizing its violence.[13] To lift the veil from a (beautiful) false surface — the enchantress — to reveal its (ugly) naked truth — the hag — is an ancient hermeneutic model for finding the essence beneath the appearance, couched in a gendered figure: the figure of woman, or more precisely, of her

sex, of sexual difference: "Il n'y a donc pas de vérité en soi de la dif-
férence sexuelle en soi, de l'homme ou de la femme en soi, toute
l'ontologie au contraire présuppose, recèle cette indécidabilité dont
elle est l'effet d'arraisonnement, d'appropriation, d'identification, de
vérification d'identité" ("Although there is no truth in itself of the
sexual difference in itself, of either man or woman in itself, all of
ontology nonetheless, with its inspection, appropriation, identification and verification of identity, has resulted in concealing, even as
it presupposes it, this undecidability").[14]

In "Brandon Teena"'s case, the revelation allegorizes the disavowal
of sexual difference, since the uncovering of a woman's sexual parts
beneath the "veil" of masculinity neither produced Brandon as truly
a woman—"his" girlfriend Lana Tisdale, for example, was unmoved
in her interpretation of "his" gender by the exposure of "his" geni-
tals—nor countered that truth. Rather, the action of uncovering and
the subsequent citations of that action in the various posthumous discursive reinscriptions of "Brandon Teena" only perpetuate the apo-
ria or impasse of the impossible choice between siding with either
the enchantress or the hag.[15] On the one hand, the murderers uphold
the misogynist and colonizing ideology of truth unveiled, fraud revealed; yet their disavowal is also necessary insofar as the stripping
away has disastrous implications for the question of the "essential"
status of masculinity in the discourse of truth. But, Spackman argues,
those who, post hoc, reconsign "Brandon Teena" to identitarian certainty also participate in a logic of both (hetero)sexual difference and
misogyny, for "what is 'revealed' is instead the 'truth' about the trap
itself: the notion of truth as something hidden (which can then be
revealed) necessarily implies a model of sexual difference in which
the woman stands as the privileged figure of absence" (34).

What is ultimately targeted in this account of the futures of "Brandon Teena" is the urge to identify, and thus stabilize, the meaning of
an event and a person. Hale writes: "The creation and maintenance of
that name as the anchoring emblem for a transgender political agenda
requires the erasure of all the many aspects of 'his' life that do not
resolutely conform to 'properly' transsexual or transgendered self-
identifications."[16] Among the aspects of the case erased, Halberstam
points out, is the way in which racial hatred constituted another mo-

tivating factor in the crime, for one of the victims—a victim nearly wholly effaced in the narrative—was the African American Philip DeVine, while one of the murderers was also allied with white supremacist politics.[17]

Yet this intertwining of multiple brutal logics of erasure reappears again and again. The historical and political appropriation of "Brandon Teena" as "known" cannot lay to rest the haunting that persistently destabilizes the anchors of identity and meaning. As Halberstam explains, if "haunting is an articulate discourse" and "a mode within which the ghost demands something like accountability," then "to tell a ghost story means being willing to be haunted" (73). This willingness to be haunted is an ethical relation to the world, motivated by a concern not only for the past but also for the future, for those who live on in the borderlands without a home. If the queer appropriation of "Brandon Teena" has been melancholic—an attempt to deal with trauma, in a sense, by refusing it as such, turning it instead into knowledge, into productive organizing—it has also been colonizing. Both gestures, the melancholic and the colonizing, have worked to foreclose how "he," as ghost, recurs in ways that are not so clear, and demands not a definition but the creation of a future where categorical definitions so dependent on gender and desire might prove affirmingly impossible and unnecessary. Using spectrality as a hypothesis, then, we might wonder what we would see and hear were we to remain open to "Brandon Teena"'s ghostly returns.

One such moment is the point at which one survivor, finding himself haunted, "listens" to the ghost and speaks its reminder. Matthew Shepard's homophobically motivated murder occurred in 1998, four years after "Brandon Teena" was killed and the year a documentary of the events—*The Brandon Teena Story*—was released; it also occurred four months after the torture and murder of James Byrd in Jasper, Texas, for being African American. In a statement bordering on the logically unintelligible, Matthew's father speaks "for" his son, whose wishes thus express themselves from beyond the grave. Tellingly, the ghostly performative ventriloquized by Mr. Shepard, as reported in the *Washington Post*, interrupts the logic of revenge and retribution animating the force of the law:

In a dramatic and surprising end to the Matthew Shepard murder case, convicted killer Aaron J. McKinney, 22, today was sentenced to two life sentences for beating the gay University of Wyoming student to death last year. McKinney accepted a deal brokered by Shepard's parents just as a jury was about to begin hearing testimony about whether he should be put to death. . . .

His son, Shepard said, believed in the death penalty for certain crimes, and had called it justified in the racially motivated murder in Texas of James Byrd Jr., who was dragged to death behind a pickup truck in another hate crime that shocked the nation's conscience. "Little did we know that the same response would come about involving Matt," Shepard said.

"I too believe in the death penalty," he added. "I would like nothing better than to see you die, Mr. McKinney. However, this is the time to begin the healing process. To show mercy to someone who refused to show any mercy.

"Mr. McKinney, I'm going to grant you life, as hard as it is for me to do so, because of Matthew . . ."[18]

Ghostly returns are thus a sign of trauma and its mourning.[19] This trauma, Derrida argues, is a "politico-logic of trauma," that "répond à l'injonction d'une justice qui, au-delà du droit, surgit dans le respect même de qui n'est pas, n'est plus ou n'est pas encore vivant, présentement vivant" ("responds to the injunction of a justice which, beyond right or law, rises up in the very respect owed to whoever is not, no longer or not yet, living, presently living").[20] This mourning is not a form of nostalgia, a longing for what is gone, but a kind of mourning that is "en fait et en droit interminable, sans normalité possible, sans limite fiable, dans la réalité ou dans le concept, entre l'introjection et l'incorporation" (160; "in fact and by right interminable, without possible normality, without reliable limit, in its reality or in its concept, between introjection and incorporation," 97).[21] Thinking historicity through haunting thus combines both the seeming objectivity of events and the subjectivity of their affective afterlife. As Wendy Brown remarks of spectrality's modality—what Derrida calls a "being-with specters" that is also "une politique de la mémoire, de l'héritage et des générations" (15; "a politics of memory, of inheritance, and of generations" [xviii–xix])—"We inherit not 'what really happened' to the dead but what lives on from that happening, what is conjured from it, how past generations and events occupy the force fields of the present, how they claim us, and how they haunt, plague, and inspirit our imaginations and visions for the future."[22]

Ghostliness and homosexuality have a long history of association, most frequently referenced in the clichéd and homophobic phrase "the specter of homosexuality." In its most virulent deployment, that specter is always lurking in an alley or behind a bush, waiting to pounce upon some unsuspecting innocents. When invoked more sympathetically, it hovers secretively around the edges of an otherwise perfectly straight and open — albeit presumably anxious — scene. Indeed, Derrida defines the specter in terms strikingly reminiscent of homosexual panic, the sense of a not-quite-visible contaminating near-presence that is also an anxious, often paranoid projection, the material immateriality I tracked through the term *queer* in chapter 2:

> Le spectre, comme son nom l'indique, c'est la fréquence d'une certaine visibilité. Mais la visibilité de l'invisible. Et la visibilité, par essence, ne se voit pas, c'est pourquoi elle reste . . . au-delà du phénomène ou de l'étant. Le spectre, c'est aussi, entre autres choses, ce qu'on imagine, ce qu'on croit voir et qu'on projette: sur un écran imaginaire, là où il n'y a rien à voir. Pas même l'écran, parfois, et un écran a toujours, au fond, au fond qu'il est, une structure, une structure d'apparition disparaissante. Mais voilà qu'on ne peut plus fermer l'oeil à guetter le retour. (*Spectres de Marx*, 165)

> The specter, as its name indicates, is the frequency of a certain visibility. But the visibility of the invisible. And visibility, by its essence, is not seen, which is why it remains . . . beyond the phenomenon, or beyond being. The specter is also, among other things, what one thinks one sees, and which one projects — on an imaginary screen where there is nothing to see. Not even the screen sometimes, and a screen always has, at bottom, in the bottom or background that is, a structure of disappearing apparition. But now one can no longer get any shut-eye, being so intent to watch out for the return. (*Specters of Marx*, 101)

Like the closet, whose very existence suggests the opening onto what is concealed, Derrida likens the specter to the screen whose structure is always already that of a disappearing appearance. The

what meaning does this phrase hold?

ghost is thus also structural. Terry Castle observes this phenomenon in relation to the "apparitional" history of the lesbian: "When it comes to lesbians . . . many people have trouble seeing what's in front of them. The lesbian remains a kind of 'ghost effect' in the cinema world of modern life: elusive, vaporous, difficult to spot—even when she is there, in plain view, mortal and magnificent, at the center of the screen. Some may even deny that she exists at all."[23] For those who live "on the other side" of the expression, "the specter of homosexuality," those who might be said to be named, "ghosted" by that phrase, ghosts are neither scary nor menacing, however terrifying the prospect of being turned into one might be. For one may also reverse the perspective and understand the specter as that which sees without being seen, as what produces the sense of being seen, observed, surveilled.[24] Hélène Cixous declared, concerning one famous gynephobic patriarchal figure of woman, "You only have to look at the Medusa straight on to see her. And she's not deadly. She's beautiful and she's laughing."[25] To be a ghost among ghosts is to "see" the ghost not as a feared and fearful projection—the way Medusa cannot be directly seen by men—but perhaps as beautiful, though rarely laughing, for the specter is the form a certain unfinished mourning takes. Thus part of what it might mean to live with ghosts would be to understand oneself as "ghosted," and to understand "learning to live" as something that takes place "between life and death" as the "non-contemporaneity with itself of the living present."[26] This would then be an approach to history—and to justice—that would neither "forget the dead" nor "successfully" mourn them.[27]

Exploring further the notion of haunting as the way history registers as affect in the social and psychic lives of beings, and the reciprocity of haunting and being haunted, Avery Gordon follows the figure of the ghost and the poetics of haunting in other contexts to understand the specificity of this way of coming to terms with historical trauma.[28] *Ghostly Matters* looks to Toni Morrison's *Beloved* to see how haunting conveys the traumatic effect and affect of the historical event on the subject and the social responsibility that is thereby entailed.[29] Thus what Derrida analyzes in the work of Marx and philosophy, Gordon studies in a kind of embodied poetics, tracking how the ghost's figurative "materialization" elicits, even as it emblematizes, traumatic repetition and working through.[30] In that process of materialization, or poetic embodiment, Hamlet's father undergoes a morphological transformation, from Danish king to African slave and from father to daughter; the ghostly exchange takes place not between a father and his son but between a daughter and her mother; and the "allegory" of haunting moves from Europe to America.[31] Like Gordon, in what follows I track a transatlantic passage from an earlier moment and an earlier historical trauma as they haunt both within and outside of their own time.

In *Premodern Sexualities*, Louise Fradenburg and I raised questions concerning the fantasmatic relationship that we, as scholars of the past and scholars working "queerly" in the history of sexuality, might affirm in relation to the past, "ours" or that of others, in the name of pleasure.[32] It was an effort, in part, to honor the complex pleasure-positivity of queer theory in its resistance to the heteronormatively disciplining discourses that came self-righteously to the fore when AIDS in the United States became associated with "homosexuals" and "promiscuity." It was also a way of examining how desires and identifications—queer theory's psychoanalytically inflected terminological legacies—are at work in historical scholars' investments in the differences and similarities between the past and the present. Finally, it was a way of noting historiography's own (self-)disciplining force, its "repudiations of pleasure and fantasy" in spite—or because—of its queer wishes (xvii); thus we argued for a queer historiography that would devote itself to a critical revalorization of the places and possibilities of pleasure within the serious and "ascetic" work of history.

Insofar as queer historicism registers the affective investments of the present in the past, however, it harbors within itself not only pleasure, but also pain, a traumatic pain whose ethical insistence is to "live to tell" through complex and circuitous processes of working through. Thus we concluded the introduction with an ethically impelled wish:

> The past may not be the present, but it is sometimes in the present, haunting, even if only through our uncertain knowledges of it, our hopes of surviving and living well. The questions we are raising about the practice of history may help us understand better the living and dying of twentieth-century bodies and pleasures. And we hope that

consideration of the ways in which historicisms are currently questioning sexuality, and sex studies questioning historicism, will work to affirm the pleasures of mortal creatures. (xxi)

The past is in the present in the form of a haunting. This is what, among other things, doing a queer kind of history means, since it involves an openness to the possibility of being haunted, even inhabited, by ghosts. What is transmitted in the cohabitation of ghostly past and present is related to survival, to "living well," and to the "pleasures of mortal creatures," survivals and pleasures that have little to do with normative understandings of biological reproduction.

Jonathan Goldberg further explores the implications of queering history in his essay in the same volume.[33] A scene in Eduardo Galeano's *Memory of Fire* describes a moment in the European invasion of the Americas where the Spanish are surrounded and victory for the Indians is imminent; Goldberg analyzes the exchange between the Araucanian chief and Bernal, where the chief predicts the extinction of the Spanish on New World territory, while the Spaniard declares that reproduction will occur and that the resulting *mestizaje* will complete the task of conquest for the Spanish against the indigenous parents and relatives of the mestizos. This is a moment when, Goldberg argues, the question of the future is at stake and the "history that will be" is suspended, opened up for multiple possibilities. For although from a position of retrospection one might argue for the prescience of the Spaniard's assertion, nevertheless the question of the "outcome" of the history that produces a mestizo Latin America is still open to an indeterminate futurity:

> To see that in this moment the history that will be is an open question, not the one foreclosed by the Spaniard and by those who have written as if he spoke with the voice of history, is to become engaged in a scene of revisionary reading made possible not simply by Galeano's text, but by its full imbrication in the multiples of history that enabled him to write in the first place. Any number of voices, now, could find themselves in the open space of implicit rejoinder. (4)

Goldberg combines a desire to unwrite the retrospection of historical accounts of the conquest with a deconstruction of the implicit heteronormativity of historical continuity, the way historical succession is tied—in Galeano's fictional encounter as in second-order historical narratives—to heterosexual reproduction. In its radical disruption of normative temporal continuities, both for what happens and for how we tell what happens, this kind of historical practice, which is also a queering of the notion of "succession" itself, aims to open up sites of possibility effaced, if not foreclosed, by (hetero)normative historicisms.

Like Goldberg, scholars of New World conquest or encounter studies have tried numerous strategies to confront ethically the event of the conquest and to do justice to the historical traumaticity of the event, both "for" then and for now.[34] Some, such as Beatriz Pastor, invoke Hayden White's study of the rhetorical modalities of historiography to note the intercontamination of historical and fictional discourses and thus to read the documents of the conquest/encounter for the way they narrate not only "events," but also desire.[35] Citing Eric Wolf's notion of "the people[s] without history" (147),[36] Pastor writes, "In the case of Latin America, to rewrite the history of its conquest . . . implies retracing the lost steps, listening to other voices that could have related the history of a discovery rooted in dreams and lies, of a New World that, through the very process of its conquest, was lost forever" (147). Here, writing the history of those without one is a fantasmatic activity that describes an impossible wish; it involves (citing Alejo Carpentier)[37] following traces that are lost, listening to voices that "could have" spoken (but, it is implied, did not), all toward the goal of describing a New World that was—and thus is—lost forever. This impossible task of retracing and listening, of locating desire in the (not quite total) silences of texts, articulates a complex interplay of desire and identification that is also Pastor's own:

> Where are the eyes that could show us the women's side of the world of war and conquest, about which so many famous historians have written so much? And where are the words that could break the silence that covers the voices of all those women who, like Malintzin, struggled in a world created and controlled by men, without even leaving a tiny scratch on the yellowing pages of so many historical documents: words that could show us what they were like as people, as women, as voices, as eyes, as tongues? (149)

Echoing the slogan of antiquincentenary demonstrations—
"Where are the Arawaks?"—Pastor invokes Doña Marina as the exemplary and overdetermined sign of a silence.[38] The multilingual
indigenous interpreter about whom so much has been written and
whose body parts and signature are continually reappropriated in
documents of the conquest (she is Cortés's tongue and he in turn is
often referred to by her name) is precisely one whose voice may be
said to have determined history without, as Pastor notes—here echoing Susan Gubar's figure of the "blank page" for women's historical
creativity[39]—leaving "even a tiny scratch on the yellowing pages of
so many historical documents."[40] Like Echo's voice to Narcissus's embodiment, Malintzin is the ventriloquized word of the conqueror,
unable to show us the difference of her "women's side of the world."[41]
It is interesting that the passage mimes the progressive disintegration
of Echo herself and of that world to which Pastor refers, for by the
end the women are disassembled into so many isolated organs of perception and communication. Yet something about this passage strains
to hear, even from within the mournful lament of a loss. Pastor enacts
a kind of automatic writing then, a practice of scratching the page as
an act of listening to lost voices. She is, we might say, inhabited by
a ghost, the ghost of Malintzin and "the voices of all those women
who, like Malintzin, struggled in a world created and controlled by
men" (149).

Tzvetan Todorov, who also experiences an ethical imperative in
narrating the conquest, also suggests that what presses upon his project—as upon the Europeans who will emerge victorious from their
encounter with the Aztecs and Mayans (for these are his main focus)
—is a silence from the past. Todorov's work has been much criticized
—most notably by Stephen Greenblatt—for an overemphasis on the
already civilizationally overdetermined opposition between "speech"
and "writing," and between "traditional" or "ritual" and "improvi-
sational," the Europeans representing the latter example in each binary.[42] Todorov argues this, as does Greenblatt, in relation to the
question, ceaselessly asked by European scholars, of why the Spanish emerged victorious from the encounter with a far more powerful empire. This search for an origin is almost always an ideological
deployment, one that seeks to displace a certain guilt in part by re-
framing the encounter as a David and Goliath story where David un-

expectedly takes the day. Indeed, for Todorov, these oppositions are radically unstable to the extent that his attempt to describe differing worldviews in the domain of communication does not serve the purpose of historical explanation. As he himself notes in the introduction, his is a cautionary tale, motivated by moral rather than historical exigencies aimed at the present rather than the past.[43] Although it may be easier for modern European secularist readers to assume that Todorov's description of Spanish interhuman communication (the collecting of information) accords it superiority over either communication with the past (the ancients) or human/divine communication (two of the ways Todorov describes Aztec intelligence gathering), the conclusion to this section interestingly turns this around:

> Les Espagnols gagnent la guerre. Ils sont incontestablement supérieurs aux Indiens dans la communication interhumaine. Mais leur victoire est problématique, car il n'y a pas une seule forme de communication, une seule dimension de l'activité symbolique. Toute action a sa part de rite et sa part d'improvisation, . . . l'homme a tout autant besoin de communiquer avec le monde qu'avec les hommes. La rencontre de Moctezuma avec Cortés, des Indiens avec des Espagnols, est d'abord une rencontre humaine; et il n'y a pas à s'étonner que les spécialistes de la communication humaine l'emportent. Mais cette victoire, dont nous sommes tous issus, Européens comme Américains, porte en même temps un grave coup à notre capacité à nous sentir en harmonie avec le monde, à appartenir à un ordre préétabli; elle a comme effet de refouler profondément la communication de l'homme avec le monde, de produire l'illusion que toute communication est communication interhumaine; le silence des dieux pèse sur le camp des Européens autant que sur celui des Indiens. (*La conquête de l'Amérique*, 126–27)

The Spaniards win the war. They are incontestably superior to the Indians in the realm of interhuman communication. But their victory is problematic, for there is not just one form of communication, one dimension of symbolic activity. Every action has its share of ritual and its share of improvisation; . . . man has just as much need to communicate with the world as with men. The encounter of Montezuma with Cortés, of the Indians with the Spaniards, is first of all a human encounter; and we cannot be surprised that the specialists in human communication should triumph in it. But this victory from which we all derive, Europeans and Americans both, delivers as well a terrible blow to our capacity to feel in harmony with the world, to belong to a preestablished order; its effect is to repress man's communication with the world, to produce the illusion that all communication is inter-human communication; the silence of the gods weighs upon the camp of the Europeans as much as on that of the Indians. (*The Conquest of America*, 97)

Here, the "silence" of (divine) voices weighs upon not only the Europeans of the past, but those of the present as well. Voices that once spoke—in the past—withhold their speaking in the present. But what is repressed (*refoulé*) threatens to return; this withholding continues to haunt.[44]

For Goldberg, the queering of the English encounters that will come to be called the conquest produces a scene in which the failed conquerors at Roanoke reproduce themselves in the future through the "invisible bullets" of disease; he argues that "in this auto-erotic scene of conjuring up the desired future, is the body of the Indian, a strange specular double for these English shooters."[45] His is a scene of homoerotic encounters between the present of the English invaders and their spectral descendants performed across the body of the Indian (man); for Pastor, the spectral body is the missing (Indian) woman in a homosocial scene of transaction; for Todorov, finally, it is the gods, or the Indian woman consumed by Spanish dogs to whom he dedicates his book. All three invoke ghosts in scenes where Indian, woman, and god mark the trace of a nonspeaking yet persistent and insistent otherness caught in, effaced or consumed by, these queer colonial encounters. What does it mean, then, for a certain narration of conquest to invoke the figure of a ghost, a ghost who clearly continues to haunt the moment of reading and writing in the present? And what does it mean that implicated in the appearance of the ghost are queered relations of gender, sexuality, race, and species?

In "Archive Fever: A Freudian Impression," Derrida remarks that "a spectral messianicity is at work in the concept of the archive."[46] Further, in a passage that makes the notion of the archive constitutively spectral and links that spectrality to the "being" of a ghost, he writes: "The structure of the archive is spectral. It is spectral a priori: neither present nor absent 'in the flesh,' neither visible nor invisible,

a trace always referring to another whose eyes can never be met"
(54).[47] Thus for these writers engaged in an ethical relation to a traumatic past event, the trace that is also a calling, a demand, a messianic
wish or hope, takes the troubled form of a ghost—neither altogether
present nor quite absent—conjured by the moment of writing. And
it is no coincidence that the figures invoked in these archival memo-
rials are racially and sexually marked, for just as ghostliness designates an ambiguous state of being, both present and not, past and
not, so too in these accounts racial mixture and sexual—including
sexuality—difference stand in for, even as they mark the material
place of, a critique of originary purity, simplicity, and unmixedness.
Fredric Jameson analogizes this to the philosophical project of Derridean spectrality, which takes aim at all that "is somehow pure and
self-sufficient or autonomous, what is able to be disengaged from the
general mess of mixed, hybrid phenomena all around it and named
with the satisfaction of a single conceptual proper name."[48]

If figures of ghostliness—one way to think spectrality—appear as a
way to relate to the past, this past is not, nevertheless, an origin, however much these discourses about conquest and traumatic genocidal
encounters might seem to suggest this. Wendy Brown writes, "the
specter reverses the usual understanding of history as origin (and the
present as the teleological fruit of the origin) by virtue of its always
being a revenant, a coming back . . . The specter begins by coming
back, by repeating itself, by recurring in the present. It is not trace-
able to an origin nor to a founding event, it does not have an ob-
jective or 'comprehensive' history, yet it operates as a force."[49] That
force, what I have been calling in the work of conquest or encounter-
studies writers an ethical imperative, is a social force and as such
places a demand upon the present, a "something that must be done
that structures the domain of the present and the prerogatives of
the future."[50] It is thus also collective, another way of thinking spectrality's specificity as historical. "History," writes Gordon, "is that
ghostly . . . totality that articulates and disarticulates itself and the
subjects who inhabit it" (184).

Haunting engages alterity; "what comes back to haunt are the
tombs of others, ancestors or affines, our own or those of others."[51]
There is no "propriety," no "proprietariness" in ghostliness; the ghost
does not, in other words, necessarily belong to those who are haunted.

[handwritten margin notes: alterity; the state of being other or different; otherness]

by it. Rather, "ghosts figure the impossibility of mastering, through either knowledge or action, the past or the present." Instead "they figure the necessity of grasping certain implications of the past for the present only as traces or effects."[52] In the writings I have been discussing, the past in question can in some sense be said to be, in spite of Goldberg's salutary resistance in particular, definitively past, and the longing or loss that marks these discourses with a certain solemnity testifies to this impression. And yet, each project—feminist, multicultural, and queer, roughly speaking—also allows itself to be haunted in the context of an articulation of political aspirations in the present and for the future. The recurrence of "indigenous" haunting articulated in their writing also signals the repetition of a prior haunting, a haunting that was both a memorial and a messianic invocation, the "ghost dance" of the North American Plains Indians during their radical displacement and destruction.[53] As Gayatri Spivak imagines it, this dance that conjured ancestors for a future to come was "an attempt to establish the ethical relation with history as such, with ancestors real or imagined."[54]

In commenting on the place from which a ghost emerges in the "cryptography" of Nicolas Abraham and Maria Torok's theories of melancholia, Derrida remarks that "the crypt is the vault of a desire."[55] Abraham, referring to the refused and unknown secret that is the encrypted phantom inhabitation, says, "this other . . . is a love object."[56] Pastor, Todorov, and Goldberg all show, in different ways, how secret mobilizations of desire and identification inspire both the ghosts in their texts and their own spectral endeavors. If desire for—and of—the other is part of what is hidden in the crypt, part of what arrives or comes back as insistent and persistent phantom, then a spectral approach can make room for, or leave itself open to, the materialization and voicing of that desire so that it might thereby appear and speak.[57]

Thus far I have been attending to the ways ghosts, ghostliness, and haunting appear as tropes or figures (of loss, of mourning, and also of a "something to be done") in discourses about a particular (and partially imagined) traumatic past, and how those figures articulate a "hauntology," a spectral approach to an ethico-historical situation. What might it mean to take such an approach—"historiography as hauntology"[58]—at a moment when the ghost—which in some ways resembles the ghosts conjured by Pastor, Todorov, and Goldberg—seems, from our perspective, to appear proleptically in the conjurings of a "colonial" European subject such as Jean de Léry?[59] What pasts return to haunt this subject in its present and what historico-ethical demands follow from that haunting? And further—as I hope to highlight in pausing on the moments when the *Histoire d'un voyage en terre de Brésil* allows itself to be inhabited by returning others—how does this haunting suggest a specifically queer spectrality, queer both in its uncanniness and in its engagement with desire?

Jean de Léry, a Protestant minister who, in 1556 at the age of twenty-two, went to the French colony commanded by Villegagnon near the Bay of Rio to preach Calvinist doctrine, found himself exiled by Villegagnon from the fortress and "at the mercy of" the Tupinamba Indians, with whom he stayed as a guest for almost a year. Upon his return to France in 1558, he began his ministry. Later Léry directly suffered the bloodiest decades of the French religious wars, including the 1572 massacre of Saint-Barthélemy. He survived by escaping to Sancerre and, in 1574, published an account of the siege and famine of that town, a Protestant stronghold where he ministered.[60] In 1578, and thus over twenty years after the fact, he published the first edition of his *Histoire d'un voyage en terre de Brésil*, claiming that it had been written in 1563 then lost, found, lost again, and found again.[61] The gap between Léry's first encounter with Brazilian land and people and his retrospective account of it is thus marked, both by loss (the inability to hang on to or preserve the recorded traces of the event) and by a shattering national event, the Saint-Barthélemy, that to this day haunts the French nation as perhaps the first "modern" moment when internal religious division precipitated mass murder.[62]

Léry's text describes a haunting that differs both from triumphant conquest narratives such as that of Cortés and from the fearful accounts of indigenous cannibalism that threatened and titillated European travelers and observers in the New World. Indeed, cannibalism is in some sense haunting's double, its evil twin. A literalization of melancholic incorporation through the ingestion of the other, cannibalism is the flip side of the excorporation that a ghost might be said to be.[63] But cannibalism participates in the fundamental "impossibility" of mourning, in that the desire to incorporate the other within the self fundamentally destroys its alterity or otherness and

[handwritten margin note: exploration is the process of through which mass cannibalized or cultural are changed or remade into ones own.]

[handwritten note at bottom: this might work for my 1 page essay for the 1st part of the book]

consequently negates the other: "Dans le deuil réussi, j'incorpore le mort, je me l'assimile, je me réconcilie avec la mort, et par conséquent je dénie la mort et l'altérité de l'autre-mort. . . . Là où l'introjection endeuillée réussit, le deuil annule l'autre" (In successful mourning, I incorporate the dead one, I assimilate him to myself, I reconcile myself with/to death, and consequently I deny death and the alterity of the dead other. . . . There where mourning introjection succeeds, mourning negates the other).[64] In both anthropological and psychoanalytic literature, cannibalism is the desire to make what is other same, to annihilate or assimilate the other by incorporation.[65]

In his account of Sancerre, Léry mentions cannibalism—exclusively in order to condemn it—in a gruesome story about starving parents who devour their daughter.[66] However evoked by Léry's New World memories, cannibalism is not, nevertheless, a practice specifically tied to those places. On the contrary, when the question of Tupi cannibalism arises, it is in the context of a comic account of miscommunication on the one hand and, on the other, a diatribe against the cannibalism exemplified by combatants in the wars of religion in France.[67] And indeed, the cannibalism that occasions such horror in Léry is European and French, not only in its location and motivating forces, but also in its style, for what is consumed is the heart of a kinsman who is also a political enemy, a gesture familiar to domestic European accounts of familial revenge from the middle ages onward.[68] Cannibalism, as a crisis of identification and desire, becomes the double emblem of a barbarous Catholicism and a civil war.[69]

Neantmoins à fin que ceux qui liront ces choses tant horribles, exercées journellement entre ces nations barbares de la terre du Bresil, pensent aussi un peu de pres à ce qui se fait par deçà parmi nous: . . . en la France quoy? (Je suis François et me fasche de le dire) durant la sanglante tragedie qui commença à Paris le 24. d'Aoust 1572. . . . la graisse des corps humains (qui d'une façon plus barbare et cruelle que celle des sauvages, furent massacrez dans Lyon, après estre retirez de la riviere de Saone) ne fut-elle pas publiquement vendue au plus offrant et dernier encherisseur? Les foyes, coeurs, et autres parties des corps de quelques-uns ne furent-ils pas mangez par les furieux meurtriers, dont les enfers ont horreur? Semblablement après qu'un nommé Coeur de Roy, faisant profession de la Religion reformée dans la ville d'Auxerre, fut miserablement massacré, ceux qui commirent ce meurtre, ne decouperent-ils pas son coeur en pieces, l'exposerent en vente à ses haineux, et finalement le ayant fait griller sur les charbons, assouvissans leur rage comme chiens mastins, en mangerent? . . . parquoy qu'on n'haborre plus tant desormais la cruauté des sauvages Anthropophages, c'est à dire, mangeurs d'hommes: car puisqu'il y en a de tels, voire d'autant plus detestables et pires au milieu de nous, qu'eux qui, comme il a esté veu, ne se ruent que sur les nations lesquelles leur sont ennemies, et ceux-ci se sont plongez au sang de leurs parens, voisins et compatriotes, il ne faut pas aller si loin qu'en leur pays, ny qu'en l'Amerique pour voir choses si monstrueuses et prodigieuses. (*Histoire d'un voyage*, 375–77)

Nevertheless, so that those who read these horrible things, practiced daily among these barbarous nations of the land of Brazil, may also think more carefully about the things that go on every day over here, among us . . . what of France? (I am French, and it grieves me to say it.) During the bloody tragedy that began in Paris on the twenty-fourth of August 1572 . . . the fat of human bodies (which, in ways more barbarous than those of the savages, were butchered at Lyon after being pulled out of the Saône)—was it not publicly sold to the highest bidder? The livers, hearts and other parts of these bodies—were they not eaten by the furious murderers, of whom Hell itself stands in horror? Likewise, after the wretched massacre of one Coeur de Roy, who professed the Reformed Faith in the city of Auxerre—did not those who committed this murder cut his heart to pieces, display it for sale to those who hated him, and finally, after grilling it over coals—glutting their rage like mastiffs—eat of it? . . . So let us henceforth no longer abhor so very greatly the cruelty of the anthropophagous—that is, man-eating—savages. For since there are some here in our midst even worse and more detestable than those who, as we have seen, attack only enemy nations, while the others over here have plunged into the blood of their kinsmen, neighbors, and compatriots, one need not go beyond one's own country, nor as far as America, to see such monstrous and prodigious things. (*History of a Voyage*, 131–33)

In Léry's account, the practices of the French in the religious wars enact a logic of revenge and carnivorous sacrifice that outstrips the barbarity of the wild people of Brazil by virtue of its pecuniary motives, and its familial, and thus intranational, character. New World tropes circulate in this passage: horror, barbarity, massacre, dismemberment, even "grilling," yet they are redeployed to describe, not the warlike and culinary practices of the anthropophagi, but the domestic practices of warfare within the French state. Further, the insistence on the terms *barbarity* and *massacre* and the comparison to mastiffs, all yoked to the thematics of greed, suggests another text whose rhetoric reversed the savage/civilized binary to produce a portrait of "native" nobility as against European barbarity, Bartolomé de Las Casas's *Devastation of the Indies*, which followed upon the *Apologética historia*. Las Casas read aloud before the royal Spanish court in the "great debate" with Sepúlveda at Valladolid in 1550.[70] The book, published in 1552, circulated widely throughout Europe; Léry mentions it in a subsequent edition of the *Histoire*, in an addition to his chapter on European barbarity, and Montaigne paraphrases from it in "Des Coches."[71] Cannibalism, for Léry, is political suicide; it amounts to eating the "heart of the king," as his play on the massacre and dismemberment of Coeur de Roy suggests. In some contexts, and notably in Etienne de La Boétie's famous treatise, *La servitude volontaire*, bad kings are considered *mange-peuples*; thus a logic of revenge might dictate the seemingly revolutionary gesture of countercannibalism that would consist of eating the king.[72] In this case, that logic is enacted by another arm of the state—the Catholic religion—against a "king"—literally, a kingly heart, "coeur de roi"—rather less earthly than spiritual ("faisant profession de la Religion reformée"). Like the death penalty Matthew Shepard's father refuses—in the name of his own son's death—the political cannibalism Léry condemns consists in putting to death, dismembering, and consuming those—family, ancestors, children—whose spiritual demands haunt the nation (a repetition of the founding French religious and linguistic genocide, the Albigensian crusade).

Instead Léry allows himself to be haunted, allows himself to live with ghosts and to dream of another order, condemning the cannibalistic order of political revenge. While both cannibalism and haunting are relationships to the past, to ancestors, and to the future, to descendants, they are fundamentally different. Cannibalism is an act of erotic aggression, however ambivalent, that effaces alterity; haunting is passive, not in the sense of a lack of activity, but rather in the sense of opening oneself up to inhabitation by the other, and it is thus attentive to alterity. Cannibalism—at least potentially—permits the demonization of the other, whereas haunting implies an ethics in relation to the other. And what haunts Léry is the other's ethical imperative, his demand.

Being haunted is also a profoundly erotic experience, one that ranges from an acute visual pleasure to mystical *jouissance*. Léry's description of Tupi warfare (chapter 14) lingers on their physical dexterity and bodily superiority to Europeans; it also privileges the efficaciousness and beauty of preindustrial warfare, praising the archery skills of the Tupinamba over and against the use of horses on the one hand and artillery on the other.[73] The description culminates in a distinctly medievalizing and classicizing panoramic portrait of the battlefield that emphasizes the pleasures of spectatorship, even as it admits that Léry and his French companion are not warriors, but rather, like the women, station themselves in the rear guard to watch:

> Surquoy cependant je diray, qu'encores que j'aye souvent veu de la gendarmerie, tant de pied que de cheval, en ces pays par-deçà, que neantmoins je n'ay jamais eu tant de contentement en mon esprit, de voir les compagnies de gens de pied avec leurs morions dorez et armes luisantes, que j'eu lors de plaisir à voir combatre ces sauvages. Car outre le passe-temps qu'il y avoit de les voir sauter, siffler, et si dextrement et diligeamment manier en rond et en passade, encor faisoit-il merveilleusement bon voir non seulement tant de flesches, avec leurs grands empennons de plumes rouges, bleuës, vertes, incarnates et d'autres couleurs, voler en l'air parmi les rayons du soleil qui les faisoit estinceler: mais aussi tant de robbes, bonnets, bracelets et autres bagages faits aussi de ces plumes naturelles et naifves, dont les sauvages estoyent vestus. (351)

I will say this about it, however: although I have often seen men of arms over here, both on foot and on horseback, nevertheless I have never taken so much pleasure in seeing the infantry, with their gilded helmets and shining arms, as I delighted then in seeing those savages do battle. There was not only the entertainment of seeing them leap, whistle, and wield their swords so dexterously in circles and passades; it was also a marvel to see so many arrows fly in the air and sparkle in the sunbeams with their grand featherings of red, blue, green, scarlet, and other colors, and so many robes, headdresses, bracelets, and other adornments of these natural feathers with which the savages were arrayed. (120)[74]

Both in relation to warfare and with respect to the religious ceremony described two chapters later, Léry and the other Frenchmen are positioned with the women as distinct and separate from the men, thus effecting a racialized gendering apart from the economy "men, women, and children" that is the repeated refrain of the ethnographer's observations.[75] This positioning "elsewhere" seems to allow Léry to articulate an erotics in relation to the Tupi men that successfully distances itself from that notorious "New World" practice, sodomy, and that also cannot quite be described as "homo"-erotic, since sameness and difference here do not line up neatly into gender-binaristic columns.

Roland Greene makes the point that for early European travelers, Brazil seemed a world of objects, and Léry's description of the Tupinamba and their "adornments" as they move into battle confirms his observation.[76] Greene notes, however, that a logic of counterobjectification is also at work in the Brazilian encounter; in the colonial lyric economy of subject-object relations, these positions are open to destabilization, from the infamous instances of a European becoming "meat," to the unsettling reversal that occurs when Léry and his companions encounter a lizard:

> Mais tout incontinent à dextre, et à environ trente pas de nous, voyant sur le costau un lezard beaucoup plus gros que le corps d'un homme, . . . la teste haussée et les yeux estincelans, s'arresta tout court pour nous regarder. . . . Ainsi apres que ce monstrueux et espouvantable lezard . . . nous eut contemplé pres d'un quart d'heure, se retournant tout à coup, et faisant plus grand bruit et fracassement de fueilles et de branches par où il passoit, que ne feroit un cerf courant dans une forest, il s'enfuit contre mont. . . . J'ay pensé depuis, suyvant l'opinion de ceux qui disent que le lezard se delecte à la face de l'homme, que cestuy-la avoit prins aussi grand plaisir de nous regarder que nous avions eu peur a le contempler. (268–69)

We saw on a little rise a lizard much bigger than a man's body . . . its head raised high and its eyes gleaming, it stopped short to look at

us. . . . After it had stared at us for about a quarter of an hour, it suddenly turned around; crashing through the leaves and branches where
it passed—with a noise greater than that of a stag running through a
forest—it fled back uphill. . . . It occurred to me since, in accord with
the opinion of those who say that the lizard takes delight in the human
face, that this one had taken as much pleasure in looking at us as we
had felt fear in gazing upon it. (82–83)

Greene examines how the passage cites and mimics Petrarch's canzone 23, the canzone of the metamorphoses, where the poet-subject
is the voyeuristic Acteon caught in his (female) object's gaze and
transformed into a stag. In this passage, as Greene remarks, "agency
and subjectivity are ceded to the lizard" (123). The apotropaic effect
that the Frenchmen have had on the lizard—it stands still to stare at
them—reverses itself and freezes them in turn: "Fort estonnez que
nous fusmes en nous regardans l'un l'autre, nous demeurasmes ainsi
tous cois en une place" (269; "We looked at each other stunned, and
remained stock-still" [123]). But while in the Petrarchan lyric the
poetic subject's self-objectification is a ruse of power, the object itself
never quite achieving agential subjectivity, Léry's text imagines instead a subjective reciprocity between human and lizard where fear
and desire commingle in a mesmerizing exchange of gazes and emotions.[77] The self-objectifying projection that consists in imagining
the lizard to be gazing at a human face as upon a beautiful surface
not only accords agency and subjectivity to the lizard, but also renders passive—and, in the lyric tradition from which this passage derives its erotic force, feminine—the human object of that gaze. As
Greene writes of Léry's impulse, throughout the *Histoire* and most
especially in the "colloquy" where Léry demonstrates his knowledge
of the Tupi language, "the kind of objectification that Columbus and
many others apply to the Indians, these Europeans adapt to themselves, dissolving their own bodies into discrete aesthetic and functional parts with a relish that suggests the unrequited desire of becoming an object" (128).

The chapter "Ce qu'on peut appeler religion entre les sauvages
Ameriquains" ("What one might call religion among the savage [*sic*;
wild] Americans") represents, in some respects, the heart of Léry's
book, for it deals with the most vexed of early modern questions

in relation to the indigenous Americans, whether or not they were possessed of religion; it is also the subject closest to Léry's own field of expertise as a Calvinist minister. At the beginning of the chapter, he declares in the strongest terms that the Tupi are utterly devoid of religion (377–79; 134); nevertheless, the chanting ceremony he witnesses—like a voyeur happening upon a sacred scene—has all the characteristics of a profound mystical experience and indeed haunts Léry in the present of writing, some twenty years after the event:

> Et de faict, au lieu que du commencement de ce sabbat (estant comme j'ay dit en la maison des femmes), j'avois eu quelque crainte, j'eu lors en recompense une telle joye, que non seulement oyant les accords si bien mesurez d'une telle multitude, et sur tout pour la cadence et le refrein de la balade, à chacun couplet tous en traisnans leurs voix, disans: *Heu, heuaüre, heüra, heüraüre, heüra, heüra, oueh*, j'en demeuray tout ravi: mais aussi toutes les fois qu'il m'en ressouvient, le coeur m'en tressaillant, il me semble que je les aye encor aux oreilles. (403)[78]

> At the beginning of this witches' sabbath, when I was in the women's house, I had been somewhat afraid; now I received in recompense such joy, hearing the measured harmonies of such a multitude, and especially in the cadence and refrain of this song, when at every verse all of them would let their voices trail, saying Heu, heuaure, heura, heuraure, heura, heura, oueh—I stood there transported with delight. Whenever I remember it, my heart trembles, and it seems their voices are still in my ears. (144)

The voices of the men, much like the (soundless) women's voices that haunt Pastor, still seem to inhabit Léry; they live in his ears, ravishing him and causing his heart to tremble, unlike the withdrawn gods of Todorov's Europeans, who haunt precisely through their (ominous) silence. While Pastor and Todorov, modern scholars of the conquest, struggle and strain to listen to silenced voices from the past—and are haunted precisely through this struggle to attend—Léry is so thoroughly penetrated by these voices that they remain with him in the present.

This line echoes in an aural register an earlier one, visual, that also uncannily describes a ghostly mode of appearance: "Finalement combien que durant environ un an, que j'ay demeuré en ce pays-là, je aye esté si curieux de contempler les grands et les petits, que m'estant advis que je les voye tousjours devant mes yeux, j'en auray à jamais l'idée et l'image en mon entendement" (233–34; "During that year or so when I lived in that country, I took such care in observing all of them, great and small, that even now it seems to me that I have them before my eyes, and I will forever have the idea and image of them in my mind" [67]). The spectral images of the indigenous Americans seem to be superimposed upon the French people Léry does, in fact, have before his eyes; they are with him in a quasi-material way, phenomenal but not fully present.

This haunting—and its relation to the present of Léry's French situation—culminates when, at the moment of departure, Léry describes his longing to remain in Brazil:

> N'eust esté le mauvais tour que nous joua Villegagnon, plusieurs d'entre nous, ayans là non seulement moyen de servir à Dieu, comme nous desirions, mais aussi gousté la bonté et fertilité du pays, n'avoyent pas deliberé de retourner en France, où les difficultez estoyent lors et sont encores à present, sans comparaison beaucoup plus grandes, tant pur le faict de la Religion que pour les choses concernantes ceste vie. Tellement que pour dire ici Adieu à l'Amerique, je confesse en mon particulier, combien que j'aye tousjours aimé et aime encores ma patrie: neantmoins voyant non seulement le peu, et presques point du tout de fidelité qui y reste, mais, qui pis est, les desloyautez dont on y use les uns envers les autres . . . je regrette souvent que je ne suis parmi les sauvages, auquels (ainsi que j'ay amplement monstré en ceste historie) j'ay cogneu plus de rondeur qu'en plusieurs de par-deça, lesquels à leur condamnation, portent titre de Chrestiens. (507–8)

If it had not been for the ill turn done us by Villegagnon, several of us, who had not only found over there the means of serving God as we wished, but had also tasted the goodness and fertility of the country, might well have stayed on instead of returning to France, where the difficulties were then—and are still—incomparably greater, with respect to both religion and to things concerning this life.

So that saying goodbye here to America, I confess for myself that although I have always loved my country and do even now, still, seeing the little—next to none at all—of fidelity that is left here, and, what is worse, the disloyalties of people toward each other . . . I often regret that I am not among the savages, in whom (as I have amply shown in this narrative) I have known more frankness than in many over here, who, for their condemnation, bear the title of "Christian." (197–98)

What might otherwise be understood as a simple and exoticizing expression of nostalgia takes on added meaning when the term *Christian* is invoked, for Léry's original mission involved his calling as a minister, and his account, at least on the descriptive level, declares the Tupinamba to be without religion. Here, then, at the purported end of his voyage, the intervening years have relativized the difference between "heathen" and Christian to the shame, on the one hand, Léry implies, of the nation (he uses the political term *patrie* in the sentence describing his love for France), and the honor, on the other, of America and the Americans.[79] Although in one respect the discourse deploys the topos of comparison in order to shame the addressees into virtuous action, in another, it refuses altogether the possibility of a better future "over here" and remains steadfast in its past and persistently present desire to return. Léry's invocation of the Tupinamba thus resists to a certain degree the opportunistic deployment of the Noble Savage as allegory or moral parable in discourses that situate themselves within a corrupt but nevertheless implicitly "civilized" and therefore superior context. Rather, in the choice between "them" and "us," he suggests that he would have chosen—and still chooses—them.

Léry's political and religious experience at the hands of his countrymen—a traumatic event to which he returns even after the account of Sancerre has been written and published—thus finds a haunting reminder in the displaced figure of the Tupinamba cannibal. But that haunting—the one performed by the Tupinamba on the person of Léry—enjoins Léry not to condemn the New World inhabitants who have become legendary in the imaginations of European travel narrative readers, but to urge upon the present and the future a halt to the genocidal practices of warfare that decimate the homeland and—we might understand by implication—the New World as well. Thus we might discern in Léry's "complaint" the formulation of an ethical imperative that articulates itself in excess of—and in uncomfortable contrast to—his providential Calvinist polemics.

At the same time, the (homo)erotics of Léry's descriptions and the erotic effects of being haunted differ from those identified by Gold-

berg in "Discovering America."[80] Goldberg analyzes the excessive deployment of sodomy in accounts of European encounters in the New
World. He points out that the alleged first letter Cortés sent back to
Spain proclaims: "They are all sodomites!" and he seeks to understand what this accusation—in its sheer excess—might signify. As he
notes, "sexuality is never simply a set of acts unconnected to questions of power" (184), and in early modern Europe at least, sodomy is
almost always connected to the question of a political crime.[81] Goldberg proposes the rhetorical figure of the preposterous—the confu-
sion of before and behind—as the logic at work in the discourse of
conquest. *Preposterous* is a figure that evokes sodomy, of course, along
with the force of its perception as a perversion of nature. *Preposterous*
is also both spatial (a displacement), and temporal (a reversal). The
conquerors use the accusation of sodomy—that preposterous act—
to rationalize their slaughter of the people so accused: these people
have perverted nature and thus deserve to be exterminated. Thus the
accusation of sodomy is a ruse of power, a post hoc construction of
a sodomitical body to justify subsequent conquest and penetration.

Goldberg suggests that what marks the indigenous man as sodomitical is also the spectacle of a pierced and porous male body, a
male body riddled with holes. He writes, "as the Spaniards see them,
these violated bodies register a resistance to Spanish violation" (196),
and thus offer to some extent "an uncanny mirror of Spanish desires,
above all, the desire to violate" (197). Goldberg pauses on a moment
of disavowed identification that might be said to precede the absolute
opposition between "them" and "us" and argues that the annihilative
energy aimed at the sodomitical male body tries to efface this identification. It is, thus, this threatening moment of identification that
triggers both the extravagant accusation and the savage acts that are
justified by and follow upon it.[82]

Although Léry's discourse also participates in the colonizing will
to know that Certeau describes and the exoticizing movement that
makes of the indigenous American a pleasurable remainder in the discourse of scientific knowledge,[83] he is not subject to the "displaced
abjection" Goldberg analyzes.[84] He does not only wish to penetrate
a (perceptually) violated body; instead, he also gives himself over to
penetration, enacting the becoming-object that Greene describes as
occurring elsewhere in his text. Indeed, in the chapter where Léry

recounts his participation in the ritual of the *caraïbes* (chapter 16), a curious reciprocity of penetration occurs.[85] At the beginning of the shaman ceremony, Léry and the other Frenchmen find themselves waiting in the women's house while the men chant in a nearby building; Léry is at first terrified by the inhuman sounds issuing from the men. Suddenly the chanting shifts, and Léry is instead drawn to the marvelous harmonies; the women and his interpreters hold him back, warning him of possible danger: "Quand je voulois sortir pour en approcher, non seulement les femmes me retiroyent, mais aussi nostre truchement disoit que depuis six ou sept ans, . . . il ne s'estoit jamais osé trouver parmi les sauvages en telle feste: de maniere adjoustoit-il, que si j'allois je ne ferois pas sagement, craignant de me mettre en danger" (399; "When I was about to go out and draw near, the women held me back; also, our interpreter said that in the six or seven years that he had been in that country, he had never dared to be present among the savages at such a ceremony: so that, he added, if I went over there I would be behaving imprudently and exposing myself to danger" [141]). Nevertheless, he takes the risk:

> Me approchant doncques du lieu où j'oyois ceste chantrerie, comme ainsi soit que les maisons des sauvages soyent fort longues . . . couvertes d'herbes qu'elles sont jusques contre terre: à fin de mieux voir à mon plaisir, je fis avec les mains un petit pertuis en la couverture. Ainsi faisant de là signe du doigt aux deux François qui me regardoyent, eux à mon exemple, s'estans enhardis et approchez sans empeschement ni difficulté, nous entrasmes tous trois dans ceste maison. Voyant doncques que les sauvages (comme le truchement estimoit) ne s'effarouchoyent point de nous, ains au contraire, tenans leurs rangs et leur ordre d'une façon admirable, continuoyent leurs chansons, en nous retirans tout bellement en un coin, nous les contemplasmes tout notre saoul. . . . au lieu que du commencement . . . j'avois eu quelque crainte, j'eu lors en recompense une telle joye, que non seulement oyant les accords si bien mesurez d'une telle multitude . . . j'en demeuray tout ravi: mais aussi toutes les fois qu'il m'en ressouvient, le coeur m'en tressaillant, il me semble que je les aye encor aux oreilles. (399–403)

> I drew near the place where I heard the chanting; the houses of the savages are very long and of a roundish shape . . . Since they are covered

with grasses right down to the ground, in order to see as well as I might wish, I made with my hands a little opening in the covering. I beckoned to the two Frenchmen who were watching me; emboldened by my example, they drew near without any hindrance or difficulty, and we all three entered the house. Seeing that our entering did not disturb the savages as the interpreter thought it would, but rather, maintaining admirably their ranks and order, they continued their chants, we quietly withdrew to a corner to drink in the scene . . . I had been somewhat afraid; now I received in recompense such joy, hearing the measured harmonies of such a multitude, and especially in the cadence and refrain of the song, . . . I stood there transported with delight. Whenever I remember it, my heart trembles, and it seems their voices are still in my ears. (141–44)

Léry makes a small opening in the wall of the men's roundhouse and, beckoning his companions to follow, enters. What begins as a voyeuristic scene of conquest becomes instead the receptive witnessing of a marvelous spectacle, one that at first inspires fear but then produces ravishment. Like the primal scene Freud describes as at the traumatic origin of sexuality, the event both terrifies and excites, precipitating a kind of crisis of identification and desire whereby the witness is both penetrator and penetrated.[86] Léry imagines penetrating the men's secret round space, only to find himself in turn penetrated through the ears by the sound of their voices.

This image of penetrative reciprocity thus delineates a different subjectivity from the one informing Goldberg's conquerors, and it suggests the "self-shattering" impulse or *jouissance* Leo Bersani describes as distinctive and resistive in male "homosexual" subjectivity.[87] Bersani, indeed, muses that "same"-sex desire might be what permits the possibility of a reciprocity that resists the annihilative effacement of the other. "Can a masochistic surrender," he asks, "operate as effective (even powerful) resistance to coercive designs?" (99). If identification with the indigenous other man is experienced by conquerors as threatening, in need of radical and thus violent obliteration for difference to be produced—and if this is, in the context of the European–New World encounter, a "normative response"—then we might say that Léry's text enacts instead a "sodomitical subjectivity" (to adapt Kaja Silverman's term),[88] a perverse, "masochistic" identification with that other he has come—even in the eyes of the French commander Villegagnon—to resemble.

In *The Melancholy of Race*, Anne Cheng argues that national identity in the United States is characterized by racial melancholia. The dominant white citizen-subject is melancholic for having "ghosted," by consuming, the racial others of the nation; the incorporated object—racialized subjects—also internalizes an impossible (white) ideal:

> On the one side, white American identity and its authority is [*sic*] secured through the melancholic introjection of racial others that it can neither fully relinquish nor accommodate and whose ghostly presence nonetheless guarantees its centrality. On the other side, the racial other (the so-called melancholic object) also suffers from racial melancholia whereby his or her racial identity is imaginatively reinforced through the introjection of a lost, never-possible perfection, an inarticulable loss that comes to inform the individual's sense of his or her own subjectivity.[89]

Cheng's work argues for a different relationship to a traumatic history of loss, one that does not simply get over it (which, in any case, fortifies the attachment to loss through the encrypting or consumption of the lost object in the self, thereby denying loss). What alternative approaches to melancholic subjectivity and its unarticulated grief, she asks, might better serve the goal of achieving social justice and allow a "working through" that addresses the interimplications of the psychic or subjective and the social?

She begins with the question, "What is the subjectivity of the melancholic object? Is it also melancholic, and what will we uncover when we resuscitate it?" (14). The attribution of melancholic subjectivity to the racialized other is a familiar strategy of the victors to legitimize their future (14)[90] and also characterizes a certain melancholic discourse of modernity in the West that shores up and retains the centrality of that Western subject of modernity.[91] Yet Cheng's question takes seriously the status of the incorporated other as object in the dominant melancholic subject and proposes a far more unsettling situation: "It is as if, for Freud, the 'object' has, for all practical purposes, disappeared into the melancholic's psychical interiority. In short, one is led to ask, what happens if the object were to return—

would the melancholic stop being melancholic? That scenario would seem to make sense except that, since Freud has posited melancholia as a constitutive element of the ego, the return of the object demanding to be a person of its own would surely now be devastating" (200n22).

"The return of the object demanding to be a person of its own" is one way to think about haunting, as the object's return and its demand emerge when one is willing to be haunted, to be inhabited by ghosts. Further, the mutual recognition, entanglement, and disentanglement entailed by this event suggest a more complex relationship between difference and resemblance, alterity and identity (or "sameness"), than (heteronormative) discourses of identity normally allow. For, in order to enable the melancholic object-other to emerge and to demand from "within" the self, there must be identification, if not identity, between the subject and object. And yet, at the same time, for that object to demand, to become (a ghost), somehow to materialize, it must have a subjectivity of its own; it must, therefore, be other/different.[92]

This fantastic model of an otherness struggling to emerge within and sometimes against the self delineates an intrasubjectivity that is nevertheless not incompatible with or absolutely different from intersubjectivity. Cheng asks, "How do we separate ontic and familial 'selves' . . . from the subject positions invented by society, culture, and politics? In fact, the very inability to tell the difference informs us that social and psychical cathexes work in collaboration. Social forms of compulsion and oppression may have their hold precisely because they mime or invoke ontic modes of identification" (27). Thus it can be said that the ghost arrives both from within and from without as a part of the self that is also—and foremost—a part of the world. Its return is, in other words, not quite material yet is phenomenal nevertheless and, much like its primary modality, affect or feeling, it is the "material and immaterial evidence" of grief (29).

To demonstrate this, Judith Butler adapts Freud's melancholic model of subjectivity from *The Ego and the Id*—the same model from which Cheng derives her theory of racial melancholia—to describe how "the social" or "the world" enters into the subject and becomes a constitutive element of its being.[93] She argues that melancholia is precisely what establishes the distinction between the social and the psychic (171) and renders "fictional" or fantastic the workings of the world within the self.[94] Like Pastor and Todorov, Butler reminds us that "what remains unspeakably absent inhabits the psychic voice of the one who remains" (196), while Cheng concludes with an ethical injunction to listen that also invokes the metaphor of the ghostly voices of the absent speaking through the living: "If we are willing to listen, the history of disarticulated grief is still speaking through the living, and the future of social transformation depends on how open we are to facing the intricacies and paradoxes of that grief and the passions it bequeaths" (29). These cautionary or injunctive insistences point to the persistence, in the present, of a melancholia that is perhaps not finally capable of allowing the other to return. Yet Léry's queer subjectivity, characterized by a penetrative reciprocity, a becoming-object for an other subject and a resultant joy or ecstasy, suggests an alternate path to the Western melancholic's incorporation of the lost other and its permanent, if uneasy, entombment within the crypt of history.

Cheng and Butler's theories of a melancholic condition that constitutes the subject through racial and sexual norms explore the "disarticulated grief" and the foreclosures occasioned by violent repudiations. Léry's nonforeclosure of either resemblance/identification or difference permits, potentially, a nonmelancholic relation to the other (and the world) such that "he"—the other—could indeed become "a person demanding a subjectivity of his own." We might, on the one hand, read the success of Léry's openness to being haunted in the work he does to denounce and put an end to civil war, the way that haunting turns him toward a reparative future. His disaffiliation from and "disidentification" with the nation—a result, in part, of his status as an already "minoritarian subject"[95]—position him elsewhere than as imperial avatar in the New World. At the same time, he does not "go native" (though there were certainly many such examples among the *truchements de Normandie*, some of whom served as Léry's interpreters), but rather returns as other, with voices in his head and ghosts before his eyes.[96] His text is thus not "salvage" ethnography, the one-way inscription and recording of a "disappearing object,"[97] but an enactment of its own difference from itself, a textualization of France through Brazil as much as of Brazil through France. Both partake of "a structure of disappearing apparition."[98]

We might also read the persistence of the ghostly demand to be heard and recognized in a story that surfaces a century later in France, when a French Tupi descendant of the sixteenth-century French/Brazilian encounters is sued for back taxes owed to the state. According to the law of *aubaine* (from the Old French word *aubain*, meaning "stranger"), "the estate of a non-naturalized citizen reverted to the ruler upon his death."[99] Captain Binot Paulmier de Gonneville returned from his voyage to Brazil in 1505 with Essomeric, the son of one Lord Arosca, in tow, the seigneur having expressed a desire for his son to "go to Christendom."[100] Although Essomeric — subsequently baptized as Binot (Gonneville's baptismal name) — was to have returned after approximately two years, Gonneville was unable to provide him with passage. Instead, he made him an heir and married him to one of Gonneville's relations. These are the descendants who are brought to court one hundred and fifty years later: "Il advint, en 1658, qu'une poursuite en payement de certains droits d'aubaine fut intentée à la famille issue du sauvage Essomeric . . . les défendeurs repoussèrent cette prétention en objectant qu'Essomeric, leur auteur, n'avaient point été un aubain venant s'établir volontairement en France, mais qu'il y avait été forcément gardé contre la foi des engagements pris, ce qui devait exempter ses descendants des taxes réclamées" (12; It came to pass, in 1658, that a proceeding was brought against the family issuing from the savage Essomeric for payment of certain aubaine obligations . . . the defendants rejected this claim, objecting that Essomeric, their ancestor, had never been an aubain [a nonnaturalized foreigner] who had established himself voluntarily in France, but rather had been forced to remain in violation of commitments that had been made, which should exempt his descendants from the taxes that were being demanded).

One of the descendants, Paulmier, who pleaded the case, had also spent time trying to set up a Catholic mission among the Tupi in Brazil. Yet here he is unequivocal and wins the day; his ancestor was kept in France by force, in violation of Gonneville's promise to provide for his return, and thus the descendants ought to be exempted from taxation by the state. This is not reparation or restitution, at least not in any positive sense. It is a "voice" that "speaks" before the law with a demand for recognition. Nor is it the melancholic logic Brown discerns in the impulse to resolve historical trauma through the "discursive structure of wrong, debt, and payment."[101] It is rather a "politico-logic of trauma" that responds to a different—we might say haunting—demand. It does not, in other words, appeal to the law; rather it refuses the law and stages its case "beyond right or law."[102]

This anecdote, the new historicist gesture par excellence, neither illustrates subversion nor containment, pointing, as it does, only to the persistence of a demand that, like Léry's queer subjectivity, suspends the difference between difference and resemblance, even as it insists on both. Léry thus did have the Tupi before his eyes in France, though he probably did not see them;[103] besides, the ones who returned with him (as ghostly *revenants*) were also *arrivants*, those who arrived and were unable, like Essomeric, to return. And, although Léry mentions seeing, the ghostly return is not foreseeable; it returns as a name, the name of the stranger.

The story also returns us to Goldberg's admonitions concerning "the history that will be" as a moment of suspension that resists the retrospectivity of *either* triumphant *or* melancholic modern narratives of "the conquest," for the process of ethnic cleansing (through systematic miscegenating rape) that the conqueror of Goldberg's tale invokes produces a far less determinate future than the conqueror imagines. Essomeric/Binot Paulmier's family "talks back" in a voice neither wholly French nor wholly "cleansed," and their rejoinders (to the law, to France) continue through to the present. What we might perceive from this moment, then, is a France *métissée*, a country not of late-twentieth-century diasporic arrivals, but one whose history of forced migrations has never ceased to speak and to demand a certain responsibility.

If this spectral approach to history and historiography is queer, it might also be objected that it counsels a kind of passivity, both in Bersani's sense of self-shattering and also potentially in the more mundane sense of the opposite of the political injunction to act. In this respect it is also queer, as only a passive politics could be said to be. And yet, the passivity—which is also a form of patience and passion—is not quite the same thing as quietism. Rather, it is a suspension, a waiting, an attending to the world's arrivals (through, in part, its returns),[104] not as guarantee or security for action in the present, but as the very force from the past that moves us into the future, like Benjamin's angel, blown backward by a storm.[105]

Notes

1 Prolepses

1 Greenblatt, "Psychoanalysis and Renaissance Culture," 210–24. See Schiesari's critique of this essay in *The Gendering of Melancholia*, 22–26. I discuss the question of psychoanalysis and Renaissance subjectivity at greater length in "Early Modern Psychoanalytics." There are many interesting defenses of the use of psychoanalysis for pre- and early modernity; the following, in particular, have shaped my thinking: Murray and Smith, *Repossessions*; Mazzio and Trevor, *Historicism, Psychoanalysis, and Early Modern Culture*; Dinshaw, *Getting Medieval*; and Fradenburg, *Sacrifice Your Love*.

2 Greenblatt writes, "The consequence, I think, is that psychoanalytic interpretation seems to follow upon rather than to explain Renaissance texts. . . . Psychoanalytic interpretation is causally belated, even as it is causally linked: hence the curious effect of a discourse that functions as if the psychological categories it invokes were not only simultaneous with but even prior to and themselves the causes of the very phenomena of which in actual fact they were the results" ("Psychoanalysis and Renaissance Culture," 221).

3 According to Dollimore, "In English studies especially the modern and the early modern have been erroneously conflated. In particular, essentialist conceptions of the self which took effective hold only in the Enlightenment, then to be subsequently developed within (for instance) Romanticism and modernism, have been retrospectively read into the early modern period" (*Sexual Dissidence*, 279). For a poststructuralist view of early modern textual subjectivity, see Cave, *The Cornucopian Text*.

4 Dollimore, *Sexual Dissidence*, 280.

5   For a range of opinions on the subject, see, in particular, Bray, *Homo-sexuality in Renaissance England*; Boswell, *Christianity, Social Tolerance, and Homosexuality*; Goldberg, *Queering the Renaissance*; Traub, "The (In)Sig-nificance of 'Lesbian' Desire in Early Modern England," "The Renais-sance of Lesbianism in Early Modern England," and *The Renaissance of Lesbianism in Early Modern England*; Trexler, *Sex and Conquest*; Richards, *Sex, Dissidence, and Damnation*; and Fradenburg and Freccero, *Premodern Sexualities*. Dinshaw, *Getting Medieval*, 22–34, discusses at length and re-spectfully the controversy generated by Boswell's work, which asserted the existence of gay community in the European Middle Ages within the context of an early period of tolerance on the part of the Catholic Church.

6   Dinshaw describes her own endeavor as "queer history" and likens its methods implicitly to the work of psychoanalysis: "And I follow what I call a queer historical impulse, an impulse toward making connections across time between, on the one hand, lives, texts, and other cultural phe-nomena left out of sexual categories back then and, on the other, those left out of current sexual categories now" (*Getting Medieval*, 1). In *Colonial Encounters*, Peter Hulme argues simply that psychoanalysis "offers the one model of reading we have that can claim to make a text speak more than it knows" (12), which might also be a way of describing queer theory's power to read normativity's "political unconscious." See Jameson, *The Political Unconscious*.

7   There have been many important critiques of the ideological im-plications of periodization in general, and the periodizing impulse that designates the Renaissance or the "early modern" as the birth of moder-nity in particular. Medievalists, for example, have pointed to the ways in which the Middle Ages perform the necessary work of difference or negativity for the construction of what is said to follow them. See Aers, "A Whisper in the Ear of Early Modernists"; Wallace, "Carving Up Time and the World" and *Chaucerian Polity*; Patterson, "The Place of the Mod-ern in the Late Middle Ages"; and Fradenburg and Freccero, *Premodern Sexualities*. On the general question of periodization, see also M. Brown, *Periodization*.

8   For discussions about the significance of the terms *Renaissance* and *early modern* and their various implications from the point of view of Renaissance/early modernists themselves, see, among others, Mignolo, *The Darker Side of the Renaissance*; Marcus, "Renaissance/Early Modern Studies"; and Gallagher and Greenblatt, *Practicing New Historicism*. For a critique of retrospective models of history that read from the point of

view of "outcomes," see, for this period in particular, Goldberg, "The History That Will Be."

9 In *How to Do the History of Homosexuality*, David Halperin conducts a defense of historicism in the name of articulating important distinctions between the premodern past and modernity. See chapter 3 of this book for a more extensive discussion of Halperin's model of progressivist history. Trevor Hope argues in "Melancholic Modernity" that recent feminist theorists of modernity posit a "regime of the brother"—to cite the title of Juliet Flower MacCannell's *The Regime of the Brother*—a modernity subtended by the presumption of a premodern, even prehistorical or primitive, homoerotic/homosexual past. See also Hope's "Sexual Indifference and the Homosexual Male Imaginary." I discuss Hope's argument regarding modernity in "Early Modern Psychoanalytics." For a critique of the paradigmatic place of the early modern period in narratives about modernity, see Freccero, "Toward a Psychoanalytics of Historiography." There have been many critiques of (the politics of) the temporality of modernity; for an overview, see Osborne, *The Politics of Time*, and Latour, *We Have Never Been Modern*, originally published as *Nous n'avons jamais été modernes*. Postcolonial scholars, in particular, have troubled narratives of Western modernity, though more often than not they have done so from "within" the modern. See, for some examples, Fabian, *Time and the Other*; Saakana, "Mythology and History"; Clifford, "On Ethnographic Allegory"; Bhabha, "DissemiNation"; McClintock, *Imperial Leather*; and Chakrabarty, *Provincializing Europe*.

10 Greenblatt's "Psychoanalysis and Renaissance Culture," discussed above, implicitly charges psychoanalytic readings with anachronism. I assert the problematic nature of claims to use only those tools of analysis that the culture under study developed for itself in *Father Figures*, an argument that finds relatively sophisticated expression in the work of Edwin Duval, among others; see "Lessons of the New World" and *The Design of Rabelais's "Pantagruel."* In *Sacrifice Your Love*, Fradenburg discusses the related "sacrificial" mandate to respect the alterity of the past as a more general attribute of historicist approaches; in a semiplayful deployment of historicist logic against itself, she asks, "What respect do we show the Middle Ages when we say that responsibility involves understanding the Middle Ages exclusively in its own terms, and then insist—in effect, if not explicitly—that only postmedieval alteritist views of time and methods of knowledge production are capable of the attempt?" (65).

11 In "Butler's 'Lesbian Phallus,'" Jordana Rosenberg argues that Butler's queer theorizing takes place "in the interstices of psychoanalysis and

deconstruction" (395), though she appears to object, along with John Guillory in *Cultural Capital*, that, as in the case of de Manian deconstruction, queer theory suffers from Butlerian discursive discipleship. I would argue that the named strands of queer theorizing in question—psychoanalytic, rhetorical—are somewhat less attributable to a master theorist than to a set of theoretical and critical institutional histories in the United States from the seventies to the nineties. See chapter 2 of this book for a discussion of queer theory and deconstruction.

12 See Christopher Lane's discussion of historicism, literary "intransitivity," and psychoanalytic reading in "The Poverty of Context."

13 I am thinking of some of the critiques of progress narratives and teleological history that have been built upon thinkers such as Walter Benjamin, in "Theses on the Philosophy of History." See, for example, Benedict Anderson on the time of the nation in *Imagined Communities*; Derrida, *Spectres de Marx* and *Specters of Marx*; Osborne, *The Politics of Time*; W. Brown, *Politics out of History*; Bhabha, "DissemiNation"; and Dinshaw, *Getting Medieval*. See also Latour, *We Have Never Been Modern*, and Chakrabarty, *Provincializing Europe*. For a discussion of alternative temporal logics, especially with regard to the question of the history of sexuality, see Foucault, *Histoire de la sexualité* and *The History of Sexuality*; Fradenburg and Freccero, *Premodern Sexualities*; Sedgwick, *Epistemology of the Closet*; Halperin, *How to Do the History*; Goldberg, "The History That Will Be," *Queering the Renaissance*, and *Sodometries*; Dinshaw, *Getting Medieval*; Fradenburg, *Sacrifice Your Love*; and Lochrie, *Covert Operations*.

14 In *Specters of Marx*, Derrida engages in a long parenthetical remark that explicates what he means by a deconstructive approach to the concept of history:

> Qu'on me permette de le rappeler d'un mot, une certaine démarche deeconstructrice, du moins celle dans laquelle j'ai cru devoir m'engager, consistait dès le départ à mettre en question le concept onto-théo—mais aussi archéo-téléologique de l'histoire . . . Non pas pour y opposer une fin de l'histoire ou une anhistoricité mais au contraire pour démontrer que cette onto-théo-archéo-téléologique verrouille, neutralise et finalement annule l'historicité. Il s'agissait alors de penser une autre historicité—non pas une nouvelle histoire ou encore moins un "*new historicism*," mais une autre ouverture de l'événementialité comme historicité qui permît de ne pas y renoncer mais au contraire d'ouvrir l'accès à une pensée affirmatrice de la promesse messianique et émancipatoire comme promesse: comme *promesse* et non comme programme ou des-

sein onto-théologique ou téléo-eschatologique. Car loin qu'il faille re-
noncer au désir émancipatoire, il faut y tenir plus que jamais, semble-
t-il, et d'ailleurs comme à l'indestructible même du "il faut." C'est là la
condition d'une re-politisation, peut-être d'un autre concept du politique. (*Spectres de Marx* 125–26)

Permit me to recall very briefly that a certain deconstructive proce-
dure, at least the one in which I thought I had to engage, consisted
from the outset in putting into question the onto-theo- but also archeo-
teleological concept of history. . . . Not in order to oppose it with an end
of history or an anhistoricity, but, on the contrary, in order to show that
this onto-theo-archeo-teleology locks up, neutralizes, and finally can-
cels historicity. It was then a matter of thinking another historicity—
not a new history or still less a "new historicism," but another opening of event-ness as historicity that permitted one not to renounce,
but on the contrary to open up access to an affirmative thinking of the
messianic and emancipatory promise as promise: as *promise* and not as
onto-theological or teleo-eschatological program or design. Not only
must one not renounce the emancipatory desire, it is necessary to insist
on it more than ever, it seems, and insist on it, moreover, as the very
indestructibility of the "it is necessary." This is the condition of a re-
politicization, perhaps of another concept of the political. (*Spectres of
Marx* 74–75)

I read this as in part a description of what it might mean to do the kind
of ethical and affectively engaged history I describe and attempt in chapter 5, after history itself has been deconstructed.

15 Goldberg, *Sodometries*, 31.

16 Dinshaw's method, as she describes it, exemplifies what I am calling queer time. She writes, "Appropriation, misrecognition, disidentification: these terms that queer theory has highlighted all point to the
alterity within mimesis itself, the never-perfect aspect of identification. And they suggest the desires that propel such engagements, the affects that drive relationality even across time" (*Getting Medieval*, 35). See
also Fradenburg and Freccero, "Caxton, Foucault, and the Pleasures of
History."

17 In this sense my project allies itself with other work being done
on affect in/and history, including Cvetkovich, *An Archive of Feelings*;
Caruth, *Unclaimed Experience*; Berlant, *The Queen of America Goes to Washington City* and *Intimacy*; and Gordon, *Ghostly Matters*.

18 See Dinshaw, "Chaucer's Queer Touches" and *Getting Medieval*; de

Lauretis, *Queer Theory*; Warner, "Homo-Narcissism" and *Fear of a Queer Planet*; E. Jackson, *Strategies of Deviance*; and Jagose, *Queer Theory*.

19   I agree with much of what Lee Edleman writes in exhorting a resistance to commonality and located-ness in queer studies and queer theory; see "Queer Theory."

20   Foucault, *Histoire de la sexualité*, 59; *The History of Sexuality*, 43.

21   Halperin notably does not use the term *queer* in his argument; he thus marks his discourse as being explicitly about the question of historical identity.

22   Butler, *Antigone's Claim*; Quilligan, "Incest and Agency."

23   Cvetkovich, in *An Archive of Feelings*, also discusses the importance of attending to the afterlife of traumas that could be seen to be "uneventful" when compared to what are understood to be avowedly historical and public catastrophic events.

2 *Always Already Queer (French) Theory*

1   Morton, "Changing the Terms," 2–3. For a more concise formulation of Morton's argument, see "Birth of the Cyberqueer," and the more recent collection edited by Mas'ud Zavarzadeh, Teresa L. Ebert, and Morton, *Marxism, Queer Theory, Gender*. The accusation he makes here depends on his specific use of the term *queer*, since if *sexuality* were the term in question, one would surely be able to refute his claim with a wealth of references, particularly from Marxist and socialist feminism. For serious replies to his objection on the topic of the historicization and theorization of desire, see, for example, the work of Luce Irigaray and, in the Anglo-American tradition, Rubin, "The Traffic in Women." Perhaps the most exemplary effort of this type, but one that focuses rather less on "desire" than on women and patriarchy, is Mies, *Patriarchy and Accumulation on a World Scale*. Morton is not objecting to these efforts, nor to those that have been done under the rubric of gay and lesbian history; rather he is targeting poststructuralist and queer work in particular, as though these latter bear little relation to or do not explicitly depend on this other work that has been done.

2   For an exploration of some of the ways *queer* performs this sort of critique, see collections such as Warner's *Fear of a Queer Planet* and *Queer Transexions of Race, Nation, and Gender*. For an introductory definitional and historical overview of queer theory, see Jagose, *Queer Theory*. See also the state-of-the-field issue of *GLQ*, *Inqueery/Intheory/Indeed*, edited

by Geeta Patel and Kevin Kopelson. Some critics who appear in "queer" collections nevertheless also express a certain antipathy toward queer theory's affinity with poststructuralism; see Patton, "Tremble, Hetero Swine!" 164–65.

3 For a history of some of these "theory wars," see Duggan, "The Theory Wars." In "Why Poststructuralism Is a Dead End for Progressive Thought," Barbara Epstein provides one of the more extended arguments against poststructuralism (particularly in relation to feminism) from a "radical activist" point of view. She also marks poststructuralism as specifically French. I first heard a similar version of the "progressive" argument for an American cultural theory purged of "foreign" (i.e., French) influences, ironically enough, from Mary Louise Pratt, in "Americanizing Cultural Theory." For a journalistic denunciation of postmodernism from a feminist leftist point of view, see Pollitt, "Pomolotov Cocktail." The proceedings of a UCSC conference that addressed some of these critiques, which the organizers referred to as "left conservatism," are published in *Left Conservatism, Boundary 2*. Judith Butler's refutation of the accusation that queer politics betrays historical materialist analyses is differently inflected but characterizes the tenor of Morton's type of critique as asserting that "the cultural focus of leftist politics has abandoned the materialist project of Marxism, failing to address questions of economic equity and redistribution, and failing as well to situate culture in terms of a systematic understanding of social and economic modes of production" ("Merely Cultural," 265). Wendy Brown, in *States of Injury*, especially chapter 2, explores feminist resistances to postmodernity as a "condition" and argues for the possibility of a postmodern politics.

4 I am speaking, for the most part, about a time subsequent to the moment when, for example, Butler discussed *queer* in the context of queer politics as a politically necessary though contingent category of identity that one occupies in part because it already lays claim to one through its injurious force as a homophobic epithet. See *Bodies That Matter*, 228–29.

5 For an argument against the creation of a "proper"—both boundaried and appropriate—object of knowledge, see Butler, "Against Proper Objects."

6 For the notion of reverse discourse, see Foucault, *The History of Sexuality*, 101.

7 See Butler, *Bodies That Matter*, 228–29; also "Imitation and Gender Insubordination" and "Burning Acts: Injurious Speech."

8 Gayle Rubin's landmark essay "Thinking Sex" might be seen to

sketch the definitional contours of *queer* used as a capacious term for nonnormative sexual identities in U.S. culture.

9 See my discussion of "queer," both as an identity politics category and as a strategic conceptual category, in Freccero, *Popular Culture*, 40–46.

10 For various ways of thinking *queer* along these lines, see Butler, "Critically Queer"; Berlant and Freeman, "Queer Nationality"; and Dinshaw, "Chaucer's Queer Touches." Berlant and Warner propose *queer commentary* as an alternative to *queer theory*, in a salutary attempt to keep the field of inquiry open and to resist categorical definition; see "What Does Queer Theory Teach Us about X?" For a critique of human rights–based discourses as discourses of enfranchisement or liberation in an international context, see Grewal, " 'Women's Rights as Human Rights.' "

11 *Immateriality* here is used in both senses: to designate, on the one hand, a phenomenon that is not material and, on the other, something that is immaterial, irrelevant, or trivial. Butler's "Merely Cultural" represents another way of framing this accusation, as the trivialization of the "cultural" in relation to the "material." She writes, "Considered inessential to what is most pressing in material life, *queer politics is regularly figured by the orthodoxy as the cultural extreme of politicization*" (270). Her response is to demonstrate the extent to which sexuality is material or, rather, has material effects. See also Nancy Fraser's response, "Heterosexism, Misrecognition, and Capitalism."

12 In *The Apparitional Lesbian*, Terry Castle takes seriously the use of spectrality in relation to homosexuality and discusses how lesbianism makes its ghostly appearance in literary texts.

13 See, for example, Butler's argument regarding kinship in "Merely Cultural," 276.

14 See Butler, *Bodies That Matter*, "Burning Acts," and "Merely Cultural," where she discusses Althusser's notion of the ideological apparatus or institution as the material dimension, and thus effect, of ideology (275).

15 Teresa Ebert, in "The Matter of Materialism," targets identity politics as well for its "cultural" and thus "false" materialism; she thus comes up with a phrase that, in the terms of my argument, would be an oxymoron: "poststructuralist identity politics" (353). For feminist critiques of deconstruction as disabling the subject, see, among others, Jardine, *Gynesis*; Braidotti, "Envy; or With Your Brains and My Looks" and *Patterns of Dissonance*. The most well known articulation of this position in black feminist criticism—an articulation that

names its nemesis as "philosophical" criticism—is Christian, "The Race for Theory." See also the exchange among Joyce Joyce, Henry Louis Gates Jr., and Houston Baker in *New Literary History* 18.2. In "Why Poststructuralism Is a Dead End for Progressive Thought," Epstein mentions some of the feminist antipoststructuralist arguments, specifically as they concern Derrida (111–12). Elizabeth Grosz addresses many of these concerns in "Ontology and Equivocation." For further applications of Derridean concepts/methods to feminism, see Scott, "Deconstructing Equality-Versus-Difference"; and Butler, "Contingent Foundations." Among recent formulations of the critique of poststructuralist feminism, see Gubar, "What Ails Feminist Criticism?" and Robyn Wiegman's reply, "What Ails Feminist Criticism? A Second Opinion."

16 Riley, *"Am I That Name?"* Riley's critique of the category—as well as various critiques by feminists of color, working-class, and postcolonial feminists that have noted that the unmarked category "women" carries with it implicit specificity (that the referent is often, if not usually, white, middle-class, U.S., heterosexual)—has by now been assimilated into most definitions and articulations of feminist theory and politics. The impossibility of invoking the subject of feminism—and the difficulties of invoking "subjects" of "feminisms"—also have something to do with French poststructuralist theory, whether it be the use of Derrida by U.S. poststructuralist feminists, the psychoanalytic critique of sexual difference by Lacan, or the writings of those designated as "French feminists" by Anglo-American feminism, in particular Irigaray, Cixous, and Wittig. See, for example, Johnson, *A World of Difference*; and Scott, "Experience"and "Deconstructing Equality-Versus-Difference." For a discipline-specific critique of what Lisa Duggan calls Scott's misrepresentation of gay and lesbian historians and historians of sexuality as essentialist in "Experience," see "The Discipline Problem."

17 Kamuf, "Replacing Feminist Criticism"; Foucault, *Les mots et les choses* and *The Order of Things.*

18 More recent debates concerning feminism's institutionalization continue to focus on the relation between its political impetus and its constitution as a field of study; these debates include, on the one hand, questions about the exclusivity or centrality of the category of gender (or "sex," as in the designation "women" in women's studies) in relation to other particularizations of identity—its relation to heteronormativity and racialization, for example—and, on the other, questions about its legitimacy as a field of study with an object of knowledge; see the special issue *Women's Studies on the Edge* (*Differences* 9.3), in particular W. Brown,

"The Impossibility of Women's Studies." Robyn Wiegman's essay on the subject, "Feminism, Institutionalism, and the Idiom of Failure," a partial reply to Brown, argues for placing the question of feminism's institutionalization at the center of inquiry; she also proposes that what she calls "identity studies" might "establish . . . the study of identity as a knowledge project that distinctly challenges the identitarian form of the university's intellectual reproduction in the disciplines" (126). This raises the interesting question of whether one might in fact be able to sustain a discipline or institution "in deconstruction"; see Kamuf, *The Division of Literature*, and Weber, *Institution and Interpretation*.

19 See Coward and Ellis, *Language and Materialism*, for a critique of structuralism's failed attempt to produce a material theory of the signifier and an argument for the subsequent success of poststructuralism's articulation of a materialist theory of signification. Both Morton and Ebert reject this notion of materialism. For a sympathetic critique of Butler and Grosz's uses of materialism that also develops a notion of "deconstructive materialism" from Derrida's *Specters of Marx*, see Cheah, "Mattering."

20 For the concept of *différance*, see Derrida, *Speech and Phenomena*, 129–60; *La voix et le phénomène*; *Of Grammatology*; *De la grammatologie*; *Positions*; *Marges de la philosophie*; and *Margins of Philosophy*. See also, for a brief definition and discussion, Audi, *The Cambridge Dictionary of Philosophy*, 234. In *The Critical Difference*, Barbara Johnson discusses, among other things, the application of the notion of *différance* to analyses of sexual difference. For the concept of "inappropriate/d others," see Minh-ha, *Woman, Native, Other*; it is cited and developed in Haraway, "The Promises of Monsters." See also Haraway, *Simians, Cyborgs, and Women*; and Case, "Tracking the Vampire."

21 In *Popular Culture*, I discuss how deconstruction works to undo binary oppositions in the context of identity politics and how this is consonant with a politically emancipatory project (59–75).

22 See Dinshaw, "Chaucer's Queer Touches" for this use of the term *queer*. In *Getting Medieval*, Dinshaw develops a notion of queer history based on "touching"; see especially 1–54.

23 On the trace, see Derrida, *Of Grammatology*, especially chapter 2, "Linguistics and Grammatology." There is a section on the trace excerpted from *Of Grammatology* in Kamuf, *A Derrida Reader*, 40–47.

24 For the critical conceptual use of *nomadism*, see Deleuze and Guattari, *A Thousand Plateaus* and *Mille plateaux*. For a feminist adaptation of the term, see Braidotti, *Nomadic Subjects*.

25 In "Homo-Narcissism," Warner identifies the fixity of the mutu-

ally exclusive poles of desire and identification as one of the important heteronormative assumptions of psychoanalysis (190–206). Butler, in *Bodies That Matter*, argues that: "In psychoanalytic terms, the relation between gender and sexuality is in part negotiated through the question of the relationship between identification and desire. And here it becomes clear why refusing to draw lines of causal implication between these two domains is as important as keeping open an investigation of their complex interimplication . . . The heterosexual logic that requires that identification and desire be mutually exclusive is one of the most reductive of heterosexism's psychological instruments" (239).

26 Kamuf, "Deconstruction and Feminism," 119.

27 Dinshaw, "Chaucer's Queer Touches," 76–77; *Getting Medieval.*

28 See also Butler, "Critically Queer." Eve Kosofsky Sedgwick discusses the relation between Austin's notion of the speech act and queer performativity in "Queer Performativity."

29 Kamuf is referring specifically, in this discussion, to feminism's critique of the subject and its desire, nevertheless, to preserve a form of the subject construed as particularizing rather than generalizing. Thus, she argues, feminism produces a kind of fetishism of the subject, which on the one hand recognizes that the subject, as such, is always an idealization and, at the same time, disavows that recognition. She perceives this at work in Butler as well, whose critique of the subject resembles her own, but who nevertheless, in Kamuf's estimation, wants to retain "the category of identity for a politics" (124n14). Leo Bersani conducts an intriguing critique of the reified/fetishized subject in identity politics, arguing apropos of the "appropriated subject" that "the self is a practical convenience; promoted to the status of an ethical ideal, it is a sanction for violence" ("Is the Rectum a Grave?" 222).

30 Although it has been argued that "sexuality" as such cannot be said to exist for premodernity—given that sexuality can be thought to have a specific and distinctive historical genesis in the nineteenth century as a product of systems of knowledge and modalities of power—Dinshaw proposes that one way to think about "sexuality" for the premodern is to define it as a "cultural structure that locates an individual in relation to his or her desire" ("A Kiss Is Just a Kiss," 206). Here I would suggest a modification of the term *individual,* which is an entity to which no premodern scholar can have access, and use the term *subject* in its stead to indicate precisely that it is a grammatical position, a place, a structure that is at stake in this exploration of the history of desire in culture. See Butler, *The Psychic Life of Power,* 10–11.

31 Vickers, "Vital Signs," 186; Menocal, *Shards of Love*. Parts of the argument that follows appear in my "Ovidian Subjectivities in Early Modern Lyric."

32 Rigolot, "Quel 'genre' d'amour pour Louise Labé?" 304.

33 J. Freccero, "The Fig Tree and the Laurel," 34.

34 See ibid. and Durling, *Petrarch's Lyric Poems*, especially 1–33.

35 Culler, *The Pursuit of Signs*, 146.

36 For the relation between normative constructions of heterosexuality and the question of identification versus desire, including a critique of the collapsing of "same-sex" desire into narcissism in psychoanalysis, see Warner, "Homo-Narcissism." In *Strategies of Deviance*, Earl Jackson Jr. argues that Freud's "On Narcissism" "presents two definitions of 'narcissism': first, a range of identificatory operations that form and refigure the ego; and second, a classification of object-choice. The former offers a potentially compelling descriptive model of the dynamic interchanges constituting psychosocial subject formations . . . the latter is merely part of a two-term typology of sexual relations, and one which is thoroughly implicated in a gender-hierarchized value system" (26). See especially 26–31 for his discussion of narcissism. For a lengthier discussion of the "queerness" of early modern lyric in Petrarch and Louise Labé, see Freccero, "Ovidian Subjectivities." For discussions about the continuities between desire and identification condensed in the term *homosociality*, see Sedgwick, *Between Men*, and Dollimore, *Sexual Dissidence*.

37 Butler, *Bodies That Matter*, 239; see also *Gender Trouble*.

38 Labé, *Oeuvres complètes*, 108. For a more detailed analysis of Louise Labé's lyric, see Jones, "City Women and Their Audiences," *The Currency of Eros*, and " 'Blond chef, grande conqueste' "; see also Freccero, "Louise Labé's Feminist Poetics."

39 Barthes, *A Lover's Discourse* and *Fragments d'un discours amoureux*.

40 Rigolot, "Gender vs. Sex Difference in Louise Labé's Grammar of Love," 292.

41 Butler, *Bodies That Matter*, 239.

42 Nickson, *Melissa Etheridge: The Only One*, 71, 137.

43 From "Late September Dogs," in *Melissa Etheridge*, produced by Craig Krampf, Kevin McCormick, Melissa Etheridge, and Niko Bolas (Island Records, Inc., 1988). Words and music by Melissa Etheridge. Copyright © 1988 Almo Music Corp. and M. L. E. Music, Inc. All rights reserved; used by permission.

44 From "I Want You," in *Melissa Etheridge*.

45 In "Political Thrillers," Tom Cohen discusses Hitchcock's signature

"bar-series" or "slash" as a prefigural nonsignifying materiality inscribing difference.

46 From "No Souvenirs," in *Brave and Crazy*, produced by Kevin McCormick, Niko Bolas, Melissa Etheridge (Island Records, Inc., 1989). Words and music by Melissa Etheridge. Copyright © 1989 Almo Music Corp. and M. L. E. Music, Inc. All rights reserved; used by permission.

47 From "I Really Like You," in *Your Little Secret*, produced by Hugh Padgham and Melissa Etheridge (Island Records, Inc., 1995). Written by Melissa Etheridge. Copyright © 1995 M.L.E. Music (ASCAP). All rights reserved; used by permission.

48 See Teresa De Lauretis's important essay on the subject, "Sexual Indifference and Lesbian Representation."

49 Irigaray, *This Sex Which Is Not One*, 197; *Ce sexe qui n'en est pas un*, 193.

50 Butler, *Bodies That Matter*, 240.

51 Kamuf, "Deconstruction and Feminism," 115.

52 Kamuf and Miller, "Parisian Letters," 126.

53 Spivak with Rooney, "In a Word."

3 *Undoing the Histories of Homosexuality*

1 Halperin, "Forgetting Foucault." The critique that follows in this chapter is based primarily on the published article version of this essay and also on "How to Do the History of Male Homosexuality." Both essays have been published as chapters of a book, *How to Do the History of Homosexuality*. Some changes have been made in the book version. In my quotations, very minor changes of punctuation have been ignored; other minor changes are indicated in brackets and quotation marks; more serious revisions are included in the notes. Citations include the page numbers from the book first, then from the essay.

When Foucault discusses sexuality in *Histoire de la sexualité*, he refers to very specific discourses of power/knowledge that produce a *scientia sexualis*, a field of truth called "sexuality": "L'important, c'est que le sexe n'ait pas été seulement affaire de sensation et plaisir, de loi ou d'interdiction, mais aussi de vrai et de faux, que la vérité du sexe soit devenue chose essentielle, utile ou dangereuse, précieuse ou redoutable, bref, que le sexe ait été constitué comme un enjeu de vérité" (76; "The essential point is that sex was not only a matter of sensation and pleasure, of law and taboo, but also of truth and falsehood, that the truth of sex became something fundamental, useful, or dangerous, precious or formidable: in short, that sex was constituted as a problem of truth" [*History of Sexuality*, 56]). "De cette sexualité, les caractères fondamentaux ne traduisent pas une représentation plus ou moins brouillée par l'idéologie, ou une méconnaissance induite par les interdits; ils correspondent aux exigences fonctionelles du discours qui doit produire sa verité . . . L'histoire de la sexualité—c'est-à-dire de ce qui a fonctionné au 19e siècle comme domaine de vérité spécifique—doit se faire d'abord du point de vue d'une histoire des discours" (91–92; "The essential features of this sexuality are not the expression of a representation that is more or less distorted by ideology, or of a misunderstanding caused by taboos; they correspond to the functional requirements of a discourse that must produce its truth . . . The history of sexuality—that is, the history of what functioned in the nineteenth century as a specific field of truth—must first be written from the viewpoint of a history of discourses" [68–69]). This is what is meant when David Halperin, among others, argues that "sexuality is . . . a distinctively modern production" (*How to Do the History*, 29; "Forgetting Foucault," 97), and when Arnold Davidson talks about the "emergence" of sexuality as distinct from something called sex ("Sex and the Emergence of Sexuality"). The claim rests on the organization and deployment of specific apparatuses of discursive knowledge/power production, such as the medicalization and psychiatrization of sex, that is, the grafting of scientific procedures onto older confessional regimes to produce truth. All further references to Foucault's *History of Sexuality* will cite these editions unless otherwise indicated.

2 See Fradenburg and Freccero, *Premodern Sexualities*, xx.

3 John Boswell is considered the most well known proponent of a transhistorical sexual identity that might be called gay or homosexual; see *Christianity, Social Tolerance, and Homosexuality* and *Same-Sex Unions in Premodern Europe*. The critiques of his position are too numerous to mention here.

4 Karras, "Prostitution and the Question of Sexual Identity in Medieval Europe." Portions of my argument here can be found in my response to Karras's essay, "Acts, Identities, and Sexuality's (Pre)Modern Regimes"; see, in addition, Karras's response to Freccero and Van Der Meer, "Response: Identity, Sexuality, and History."

5 Foucault, *The History of Sexuality*, 43; Halperin, "Forgetting Foucault," 95; Halperin's modified translation. As Michael Lucey's translation of this passage indicates, Halperin continues to mistranslate "relaps" as "temporary aberration"; Lucey translates it more accurately as "re-

lapsed heretic." See Eribon, "Michel Foucault's Histories of Sexuality," 48. "Backslider" might also convey more accurately the sense of the word. In the book, Halperin omits the portion of the quotation that describes a model of spiritual hermaphroditism for the emergence of the nineteenth-century homosexual. As discussed later in this chapter, Sedgwick points out that this model differs significantly from Halperin's.

6 Halperin remarks, "As almost always in *The History of Sexuality*, Foucault is speaking about discursive and institutional practices, not about what people really did in bed or what they thought about it. He is not attempting to describe popular attitudes or ["private"] emotions, much less is he presuming to convey what actually went on in the minds of different historical subjects when they had sex" (*How to Do the History*, 29; "Forgetting Foucault," 97). In this essay, Halperin blames premodernists rather than modernists for too literally interpreting Foucault's distinction and therefore taking issue with it.

7 Eribon, "Michel Foucault's Histories of Sexuality," 52. In *Histoire de la sexualité*, Foucault puts forth the hypothesis that the reason power is most often conceived in juridico-political terms is because of the development of medieval and early modern monarchical systems: "Le droit n'a pas été simplement une arme habilement maniée par les monarques; il a été pour le système monarchique son mode de manifestation et la forme de son acceptabilité. Depuis le Moyen Age, dans les sociétés occidentales, l'exercice du pouvoir se formule toujours dans le droit" (115; "Law was not simply a weapon skillfully wielded by monarchs; it was the monarchic system's mode of manifestation and the form of its acceptability. In Western societies since the Middle Ages, the exercise of power has always been formulated in terms of law" [87]). "L'histoire de la monarchie et le recouvrement des faits et procédures de pouvoir par le discours juridico-politique ont été de pair" (116; "The history of the monarchy went hand in hand with the covering up of the facts and procedures of power by juridico-political discourse" [88]).

8 Foucault, *Histoire de la folie à l'âge classique*. See Eribon, "Michel Foucault's Histories of Sexuality," 36, 48. The translated excerpts are from Eribon, *Michel Foucault*, and *Les études gay et lesbiennes*.

9 Hocquenghem, *Le désir homosexuel* and *Homosexual Desire*.

10 Eribon, "Michel Foucault's Histories," 62–65.

11 Sedgwick, *Epistemology of the Closet*; Lochrie, *Covert Operations*; Karras, "Prostitution and the Question of Sexual Identity in Medieval Europe."

12 Foucault, *Histoire de la sexualité*, 59 (my brackets); *The History of*

Sexuality, 43; Halperin, *How to Do the History*, 27; "Forgetting Foucault,"
95; Halperin's modified translation (I have inserted "her" in the brackets).

13 Sedgwick, *Epistemology of the Closet*, 1. In his introduction to *How to Do the History*, Halperin addresses Sedgwick's critique of his work (12–13). Later on in the introduction he suggests that she targets his historicism as problematic: "Such a claim about the simultaneity of temporally disjunct historical experiences, and thus about historical difference within the present itself, was already implicit in Sedgwick's discursive critique of the notion of 'homosexuality as we know it today,' which sought to break apart the unity of that supposedly 'modern' concept and to promote an atemporal approach to contradictions in sexual discourses" (18). My own understanding differs in that I do not read Sedgwick as promoting an "atemporal" approach per se, but rather cautioning historians of sexuality against the attempt to produce a progressive or teleological account of the relation between the past and the present.

14 Karras, "Prostitution," 170.

15 See Sedgwick, *Epistemology of the Closet*, 47.

16 This is perhaps most striking in the epic poem *La chanson de Roland*. See Kinoshita, " 'Pagans Are Wrong and Christians Are Right.' " For a discussion of medieval sexuality in the context of saints' lives, see, among others, Gaunt, "Straight Minds/'Queer' Wishes in Old French Hagiography."

17 Karras's argument seems to be borne out by the criminal records of early modern Italy and France. See Davis, *Fiction in the Archives*; Ruggiero, *The Boundaries of Eros*; and Brucker, *The Society of Renaissance Florence*.

18 See Sedgwick, *Epistemology of the Closet*, 44–48. See also Eribon, "Michel Foucault's Histories of Sexuality" (quoting a 1978 interview with Foucault): " 'Once homosexuality became a medicopsychiatric category in the second half of the nineteenth century, it is striking to me that it was immediately analyzed and rendered intelligible in terms of hermaphrodism. That is how a homosexual, or that is the form in which the homosexual, enters into psychiatric medicine: the form of the hermaphrodite' " (48).

19 Sedgwick, *Epistemology of the Closet*, 45.

20 In *How to Do the History*, Halperin modifies the passage beginning "Whatever . . ." significantly, arguing instead that "There may well be modern categories of deviance—and there may well be contemporary forms of sexual rebellion, transgression, or affirmation—that correspond in some ways to the ancient figure of the *cinaedus* or *kinaidos*. But such

categories would only partly overlap with the category of 'the homosexual' . . . To capture the defining features of the *kinaidos*, it is necessary to begin, at least, by situating him in his own conceptual and social universe, as I have tried to do here" (37). Thus he takes into account Sedgwick's critique by softening the assertion of absolute temporal disjunction and supersession.

21 In the book, Halperin replaces the passage beginning "The kinaidos has not as yet . . ." with "One significant difference between the *kinaidos* and 'the homosexual' is that the *kinaidos* was defined more in terms of gender than in terms of desire. For whether he was imagined in universalizing or minoritizing terms, the *kinaidos* in any case offended principally against the order of masculinity, not against the order of heterosexuality. As such, the *kinaidos* does not represent a salient example of deviant sexual subjectivity" (37).

22 Halperin, *How to Do the History*, 109; "How to Do the History," 91.

23 Halperin, *How to Do the History*, 109 ("in the present day" is missing); "How to Do the History," 91; Sedgwick, *Epistemology of the Closet*, 47.

24 To digress for a moment, were one to do a brief survey of popular culture, one would see that for dominant culture, at least, gender has not lost its profound definitional hold on male homosexuality. Indeed, when Halperin engages in this taxonomizing impulse, he seems not to countenance Foucault's own argument regarding the nineteenth-century (and thus "modern") homosexual that he is characterized by an "interior androgyny," or a "hermaphroditism of the soul," both terms that suggest a combined gender and sexual identity.

25 Sedgwick, *Epistemology of the Closet*, 45.

26 Spillers, "Interstices: A Small Drama of Words," 79. Spillers is discussing sexuality in a very different context, one not necessarily in dialogue with Foucault. Part of her argument is that sexuality—as an "intellectual/symbolic structure of ideas that purport to describe, illuminate, reveal, and valorize the truth about its subject" (74), in short, as a discourse—nowhere touches the black woman, and that whereas the black woman is indeed, and ubiquitously, a subject of sex, she "disappears" as a subject of sexuality (76). In her recent collection of interviews, *Longing to Tell*, Tricia Rose begins to approach the question of black women's sexuality by assembling an archive from which one might develop such a discourse. On the use of "archive" in this sense, see Cvetkovich, *An Archive of Feelings*. See also Poovey, *Uneven Developments*.

27 Grosz, "Bodies and Pleasures in Queer Theory," 225.

28 Fabian, *Time and the Other*.

29 Halperin addresses this criticism at some length in the introduction to *How to Do the History* with reference to his earlier work *One Hundred Years of Homosexuality*. He notes his ongoing allegiance to his argument regarding "modern homosexuality," but he recognizes its weakness as an "unfortunate formulation," in part because "it misleadingly implies a Eurocentric progress narrative, which aligns modernity, Western culture, metropolitan life, bourgeois social forms, and liberal democracies with 'sexuality' (both homo- and hetero-), over against premodern, non-Western, non-urban, non-white, non-bourgeois, non-industrialized, non-developed societies, which appear in this light comparatively backward, not to say primitive, innocent as they are of the 'sexuality' which is one of the signatures of Western modernity" (13–14). He devotes a section to these objections (17–21). While refining his earlier claims for the modern homosexual, Halperin nevertheless seems to continue to adopt an object/other-oriented anthropological stance toward the past and to merge space and time in the manner Fabian analyzes.

30 Rofel, "Qualities of Desire"; Altman, "Global Gaze/Global Gays."

31 Fradenburg, in an extended critique of current historicist "alteritisms," highlights some of the stakes of this move when applied to temporality: "To construct knowledge about a time is to make that time past, to put it behind us" (*Sacrifice Your Love*, 51).

32 For a more developed critique of this particular move to separate gender from sexuality on the part of some queer theory, see Butler, "Against Proper Objects." See also Lochrie, "Don't Ask, Don't Tell," 149–50, and *Covert Operations*.

33 Apuleius, *Metamorphoses*, vol. 2, book IX, chapters 4–28. The story in question occurs in chapters 14–29, pp. 150–79. Boccaccio, *Decameron*, vol. 2, day V, story 10, 105–17; for the English translation, see the John Payne translation of the *Decameron*, 1:433–44; 3:867–68. All citations will be taken from these editions. For possible alternative sources for Boccaccio's version of the story, see Stocchi, "Un antecedente latino-medievale di Pietro di Vinciolo."

34 Halperin defines sexual subjectivity as a "heavily psychologized model" that "knits up desire, its objects, sexual behavior, gender identity, reproductive function, mental health, erotic sensibility, personal style, and degrees of normality or deviance into an individuating, normativizing feature of the personality called 'sexuality' or 'sexual orientation'" (*How to Do the History*, 29; "Forgetting Foucault," 97). Thus his definition combines both identity and subjectivity.

35 Close historical scrutiny of what is now a relative wealth of historical material from, especially, early modern continental Europe published and analyzed by social historians would have complicated or rendered more problematic both Foucault's and Halperin's arguments; see in particular, Trexler, *Sex and Conquest*; Brucker, *The Society of Renaissance Florence*; Ruggiero, *The Boundaries of Eros*; and Rocke, *Forbidden Friendships*. Halperin does cite Rocke.

36 Walters, "'No More Than a Boy.'" For the concept of "ideologeme," see Jameson, *The Political Unconscious*, esp. 76.

37 Walters, "'No More Than a Boy,'" 23; *Metamorphoses*, vol. 2, book IX, chapter 27, pp. 176–77.

38 The story is told by Dioneo, who often violates the decorum of the group, as he threatens to do at the end of the tenth story with his infinite reservoir ("io ne so più di mille" [120; "I know more than a thousand," 443]) of equally "bawdy" songs. As Susan Gaylard notes in "The Crisis of Word and Deed," these *ciance* have the potential to overwhelm the *Decameron* itself, which has only one hundred tales. For Dioneo's complex role in relation to the interplay of subversion and containment in the *Decameron*, see Ascoli, "Pyrrhus' Rules," 16.

39 Walters explains at length the distinction between *boy* and *man* that is partly at stake in this story. Further, several passages in the tale make clear that issues of property and adult citizen-subject status are at stake. The baker's comment, "non sum barbarus," "I am not barbarous" (*Metamorphoses* 2:176–77), puns on the contrast between himself and the fuller in the previous story about an adulterous wife; that husband, whose name is Barbarus, loses his composure and threatens to kill the young lover. In the baker's sarcastic address to the "pulchellum puellum" (pretty little boy), he invokes terms that indicate that the offense committed involves property, specifically the wife's usurpation of her husband's *auctoritas*: "'Sed nec aequitas ipsa patitur habere plus auctoritatis uxorem quam maritum'" (176–78; "'But the principle of equity does not permit a wife to have greater right of ownership than her husband'" [177–79]). For the distinction in Renaissance Venice, see Ruggiero, *The Boundaries of Eros*, 121–23.

40 Trexler, in *Sex and Conquest* (37), points out that such male-male sexual punishment—part of a more general regime of "penetrative penality," as he calls it—has been a widespread practice in Mediterranean cultures from antiquity on. He argues that such punishment is most often applied in cases of theft and especially the theft of female property that is called adultery.

41 At the beginning of his narration, Dioneo remarks: " 'Io non so s'io mi dica che sia accidental vizio e per malvagità di costume ne' mortali sopravenuto, o se pure è della natura peccato' " (105–6; " 'I know not whether to say if it be a casual vice, grown up in mankind through perversity of manners and usances, or a defect inherent in our nature" [433]). Although he is referring to the tendency people have to laugh at bad things, his suggestive formulation echoes strikingly versions of the nature-versus-nurture debate with regard to homosexuality. Such a reading of Dioneo's suggestive formulation casts considerable doubt on Walters's argument, which stresses that Pietro's "orientation" is considered "unnatural" (by Boccaccio). Rather, given this passage, the text seems all the more to be describing a version of "modern" homosexuality as Halperin defines it. I thank Albert Ascoli for drawing this phrase to my attention. On possible distinctions between deviancy and normativity, see note 46.

42 In a long note to this sentence (*How to Do the History*, 168–69n43; "Forgetting Foucault," 118–19), Halperin elaborates on this point: "A 'sexuality' in the modern sense would seem to require considerably more than same-sex object-choice, more even than conscious erotic preference. In particular, 'homosexuality' requires ["requires, first of all,"] that ["homosexual"] object-choice itself function as a marker of difference, of social and sexual deviance, independent of the gender identification or sexual role (active or passive) performed or preferred by the individual; it also requires homosexual object-choice to be connected with a psychology, an inner orientation of the individual, not just an aesthetics or a form of erotic connoisseurship." This definition, it seems to me, could never be derived from a single text, especially not one where the normativity of the narrating subject were in question, or a text where subjective perspectives were explicitly at stake in the narration as is the case in the (multiply) narratively framed short stories he analyzes in this essay. By the end of the footnote, one surmises that what is truly at stake, in this highly exclusionary definition of homosexuality, is a certain political accountability: "In the absence of the distinctively modern set of connections linking sexual object-choice, inner orientation, and deviant personality with notions of identity and difference, the substantive category of 'homosexuality' dissolves . . . and homosexually active but otherwise non-gay-identified men escape interpellation by the category of 'homosexuality' " (169n43).

43 Trexler, *Sex and Conquest* (19, 24), and Ruggiero, *The Boundaries of*

Eros, both uphold this distinction (between men and "not fully men" or "unmen") for early modern Europe, Spain and Italy in particular, from the fourteenth through the sixteenth centuries.

44 Hartley, *The Go-Between*. Here, then, is another example of a pre-modernist applying the notion of spatial and therefore cultural difference to temporality or the difference between the past and the present.

45 "How to Do the History," 90. This discussion appears in *How To Do the History* (106–9), but there Halperin does not use the suspect term *historical evolution*; he refers, instead, to the practice of "genealogy."

46 *How to Do the History*, 39; "Forgetting Foucault," 106. Walters does the same but is more specific in his claims, both marshaling evidence to support his arguments about the proscription of homosexuality in the Middle Ages and asserting the likely existence of northern Italian urban sodomitic subcultures in the fifteenth century. The most comprehensive study of sodomy in Florence is Rocke, *Forbidden Friendships*. See Ruggiero, *Boundaries*, on some of the historical problems associated with categorizing deviancy in relation to the law, which is the source of most of these records of sexual activity. In fourteenth- and fifteenth-century Venice, "illicit" sexuality (punishable by law) included fornication, adultery, rape, sex with nuns, and sodomy—yet, as Ruggiero notes, they differed in their degrees of deviation (if punishment is used as a measure) and, importantly, there was a gap between what was juridically regarded as deviant (in Venice, this would be what the ruling oligarchy regarded as deviant) and what may be inferred about normativity from the sexual practices of people. The prevalence of some of these practices—and the court's eagerness to legislate against them—suggest a more complex picture of the question of normativity and deviation (or perversion). Trexler's study supports the notion that "gender role," or status, was a more significant determinant for deviance than sexual "preference"; thus, for example, the insertive male partner in same-sex sex acts might not be regarded as socially deviant, although he might be punished for his act.

47 Ruggiero, *The Boundaries of Eros*, 137; and Stocchi, "Un antecedente latino-medievale di Pietro di Vinciolo," 352; see also editor Vittore Branca's notes to the story, especially 117n2. Gaylard discusses this in "The Crisis of Word and Deed," 40. All three also mention the fact that "Ercolano," Pietro's friend in the story, was a very common name in Perugia. Ruggiero, citing a paper by Sara Blanshei, also notes that punishments for sodomy changed in the early fourteenth century in Peru-

gia, replacing milder penalties with the more severe "burning" associated with sodomy punishment elsewhere in Italy (*The Boundaries of
Eros*, 193n77).

48 Branca notes the status of the Vinciolo family (*Decameron* 2:106).
Sodomy seems to have been very visibly practiced by noblemen both in
Florence and in Venice. Indeed, the caution and seriousness with which
the governments of Florence and Venice proceeded in sodomy prosecu-
tions demonstrated an uneasy awareness of the degree to which it was a
crime committed by peers. See Brucker, *The Society of Renaissance Florence*,
201–6; and Ruggiero, *Boundaries*, 127–29.

49 Gaylard, "The Crisis of Word and Deed," 39–40; Stocchi, "Un antecedente latino-medievale di Pietro di Vinciolo," 353. The relevant Biblical passage is Genesis 19:24, "The Lord rained down burning sulfur on
Sodom and Gomorrah."

50 In the memoirs of conquistadores, which often decry the "abhor-
rent" practice of sodomy (though it is unnamed as such), indigenous
women are invoked as disapproving of indigenous men's sodomitic practices. See Trexler, *Sex and Conquest*, and Goldberg, *Sodometries*.

51 Ruggiero notes, as do many social historians of early modern
Mediterranean culture, that Venetian authorities made a distinction between the active and the passive partner in male-male sexual relations
and that this distinction corresponded to an insertor/insertee distinction, whether the penis was inserted into the anus or between the thighs.
Ruggiero regards Venice as atypical in its severe treatment of the "active"
partner and its more lenient treatment of the passive partner (*The Boundaries of Eros*, 121), but Trexler makes the point that gender as well as sexuality is operative in the perception of the difference between these roles.
He thus would argue that Venice was typical in regarding the "active"
partner as the more culpable perpetrator (because he is the more "active"
or "masculine" agent), while greater social derision is reserved for the
passive partner, whom Trexler argues gets likened to women or to those
men whose gender status is troubled by their subservience, passivity, or
dependence upon other men (*Sex and Conquest*, 31–35). Ruggiero seems
to prove Trexler's point when he notes that in one of his case studies,
the passive partner's punishment was to have his nose cut off, a punishment normally reserved for women convicted of certain lesser crimes
(*The Boundaries of Eros*, 122). Thus it might be argued that the Boccaccio-
narrator is in fact more deviant or perverse than Pietro on the grounds
of his nonnormative gendering.

52 The quotation is from Sedgwick, *Epistemology of the Closet*; see also Lochrie, "Don't Ask, Don't Tell."

53 In *Fearless Speech*, edited by Joseph Pearson, Foucault, in a transcription of a seminar delivered in English, says, "What I intended to analyze in most of my work was neither past people's behavior (which is something that belongs to the field of social history), nor ideas in their representative values. What I tried to do from the beginning was to analyze the process of 'problematization'—which means: how and why certain things (behavior, phenomena, processes) became a problem" (171). Halperin's introduction to *How to Do the History* confirms his own (anti-Foucauldian) taxonomic project: "Even today there remain important differences in global patterns of same-sex sexual practice, and they need to be accounted for, both culturally and historically, not denied. It remains an interesting and enlightening exercise to describe systematically their differences" (21).

54 Halperin, *How to Do the History*, 135, 134, 136; "How to Do the History," 113, 112, 114.

55 For some recent discussions of the importance of gender in transgender and transsexuality, see, in particular, Halberstam, *Female Masculinity*, and *The Transgender Issue*, a special issue of *GLQ* edited by Susan Stryker. See also, for a sustained analysis of transsexual gendered and sexed subjectivity, Prosser, *Second Skins*.

56 Sedgwick, *Epistemology of the Closet*, 71, 9.

4 *Queer Nation*

1 Goldberg, *Sodometries*, 31.

2 Foucault, *Histoire de la sexualité* and *The History of Sexuality*. See also W. Brown, *States of Injury* and *Politics out of History*; Stoler, *Race and the Education of Desire*; and Halperin, *How to Do the History*.

3 Althusser, "Ideology and Ideological State Apparatuses."

4 Foucault, *The History of Sexuality*, 92–102.

5 For some discussions of the relation between nationalisms and feminisms, see Mosse, *Nationalism and Sexuality*; Jayawardena, *Feminism and Nationalism in the Third World*; Parker, Russo, Sommer, and Yaeger, *Nationalisms and Sexualities*; and Balakrishnan, *Mapping the Nation*.

6 Lucey, *The Misfit of the Family*.

7 See ibid., 13–14. Lucey notes that the legislation for the PACS was

published in *Le journal officiel. Lois et décrets*, no. 265 (November 16, 1999), 16959, and that the French Queer Resources Directory Web site (www .france.qrd.org) includes a dossier of the debates surrounding PACS. See also Borrillo, Fassin, and Iacub, *Au-delà du PACS*.

8 Borneman, "Until Death Do Us Part," 229.

9 Engels, *The Origin of the Family, Private Property and the State*.

10 For a further discussion of family and sovereignty in sixteenth-century France, especially as they relate to the life and work of Marguerite de Navarre, see Freccero, "Marguerite de Navarre and the Politics of Maternal Sovereignty" and "Archives in the Fiction."

11 Hanley, "Family and State in Early Modern France," 54.

12 From Gratian, *Decretum Gratiani*, cited in Hanley, "Family and State in Early Modern France," 54. See also Gottlieb, "The Meaning of Clandestine Marriage"; Donahue, "The Canon Law on the Formation of Marriage"; and Noonan, "Marriage in the Middle Ages."

13 Coras, it should also be mentioned, later became chancellor of Toulouse for the Protestant queen of Navarre, Marguerite de Navarre's daughter, Jeanne.

14 Davis, *The Return of Martin Guerre*, 46–47; see also Ruggiero, *The Boundaries of Eros*, for documentation of similar informal marital practices in early modern Venice.

15 Hanley, "Family and State in Early Modern France," 55.

16 Hanley, "The Monarchic State in Early Modern France"; see also Hanley, "La loi salique."

17 Hanley, "The Monarchic State in Early Modern France," 109.

18 Ibid., 110.

19 Daston and Park, "The Hermaphrodite and the Orders of Nature." See also their book *Wonders and the Order of Nature*.

20 See Jackson, "Peers of France and Princes of the Blood."

21 For the coarticulation of nation and sex more generally, see Mosse, *Nationalism and Sexuality*, and Parker, Russo, Sommer, and Yaeger, *Nationalisms and Sexualities*.

22 Another way to read the relationship articulated would be to equate the nation with woman's body—and indeed there is a long history of such associations. I deliberately here read against the grain of commonsense metaphorical associations by suggesting that, in a more literal reading, we have the king begetting sons on inert matter or, as the maxim "they are the children of the French people and the kingdom" suggests, a strange—one might say queer—threesome involving the king, the French people, and the kingdom. Thus the French people,

in a heteronormative reproductive arrangement, might also be seen to occupy the position of woman. This latter reading is one Marguerite de Navarre seems to exploit in novella 42. See Freccero, "Practicing Queer Philology with Marguerite de Navarre."

23 Sedgwick, *Between Men*; see also Goldberg, "The History That Will Be."

24 Freccero, "Archives in the Fiction."

25 Ferguson, "Recreating the Rules of the Games," 178.

26 For a lengthier discussion of these circumstances, see Freccero, "Marguerite de Navarre and the Politics of Maternal Sovereignty," "Margaret of Navarre," and "Archives in the Fiction."

27 Marguerite de Navarre, *L'heptaméron*, 290; *The Heptameron*, 385. Subsequent page references to the *Heptameron* will be indicated in parentheses with the French first.

28 For a discussion of the thematics of nationalism in story 42, see Freccero, "Practicing Queer Philology with Marguerite de Navarre." For the relation between nationalism and literature in sixteenth-century France and in Marguerite de Navarre's *Heptameron*, see Hampton, *Literature and Nation in the Sixteenth Century*.

29 For a reading of story 30 that focuses on its subtexts—which are numerous and include Masuccio, Bandello, and Luther—as well as its religious and moral content, see Cazauran, "La trentième nouvelle de l'*Heptaméron*." On incest in the period and in narrative fiction, see Archibald, *Incest and the Medieval Imagination*. Archibald discusses story 30 briefly and also discusses its departures from Bandello and Luther (140–44); see also Boehrer, *Monarchy and Incest in Renaissance England*.

30 Klapisch-Zuber, *Women, Family, and Ritual in Renaissance Italy*; see chapter 6, "The 'Cruel Mother': Maternity, Widowhood, and Dowry in Florence in the Fourteenth and Fifteenth Centuries," 117–31.

31 Lévi-Strauss, *Les structures élémentaires de la parenté* and *The Elementary Structures of Kinship*. Subsequent page references to this text will be indicated in parentheses with the French first. For a critique of Lévi-Strauss's discussion of the nature/culture divide, see Derrida, "Structure, Sign, and Play in the Discourse of the Human Sciences." See also Butler, *Antigone's Claim*, especially 15–20.

32 Similar dynamics are at work in story 10; see Freccero, "Rape's Disfiguring Figures."

33 Here the French is more pointed, deploying the reciprocal form of the verb that also suggests its reflexivity, while marking what they have between them as friendship and "resemblance."

34   Cited in *L'heptaméron*, 475 n. 526. The translation is mine.

35   Freccero, "Marguerite de Navarre and the Politics of Maternal Sovereignty."

36   My use of Lévi-Strauss throughout seeks to highlight not the structuralist rigidity of his schema, but the more figurative, or literary, of his formulations. My use of his text thus constitutes a (tacit) reading, as is indicated by the focus on his articulation of "fantasy" and his use of the word *dream* for desire; see also Lévi-Strauss, *Les structures élémentaires de la parenté*, 569 (*The Elementary Structures of Kinship*, 496–97).

37   Rubin, "The Traffic in Women"; see also Rubin's interview with Judith Butler, "Sexual Traffic."

38   Butler, *Bodies That Matter* and *The Psychic Life of Power*.

39   Irigaray, *This Sex Which Is Not One*. See, in particular, chapters 8 and 9.

40   Note that the French says "le regret de l'inceste" rather than "the incest urge." Thus Lévi-Strauss is noting "symbolic" situations where the incest "urge" is a nostalgic fantasy.

41   "Moreover, one can see in the work of Lévi-Strauss the implicit slide between his discussion of kinship groups, referred to as clans, and his subsequent writing on race and history in which the laws that govern the reproduction of a 'race' become indissociable from the reproduction of the nation. . . . he implies that cultures maintain an internal coherence precisely through rules that guarantee their reproduction, and though he does not consider the prohibition of miscegenation, it seems to be presupposed in his description of self-replicating cultures" (Butler, *Antigone's Claim*, 74).

42   Ibid., 72.

43   Butler details the ways Antigone has been taken up as example or representative, by Hegel, by Irigaray, and by Lacan, among others. The early part of *Antigone's Claim* is devoted, in part, to a refutation of the specific ways Antigone is made to signify representatively by these thinkers. Toward the end of chapter 1, she writes, "Antigone represents not kinship in its ideal form but its deformation and displacement, one that puts the reigning regimes of representation into crisis and raises the question of what the conditions of intelligibility could have been that would have made her life possible" (24). Near the end of the book, Butler writes, "Although not quite a queer heroine, Antigone does emblematize a certain heterosexual fatality that remains to be read" (72). It is in this sense, then, that I say Butler makes of Antigone a "negative" example, an example of a certain negativity that, in bringing heterosexuality to crisis,

has the potential to "raise questions" and "open up" other conditions of possibility.

44 Quilligan, "Incest and Agency," 214.

45 Goldberg surveys these various readings of Elizabeth; the "bisexed" two-bodies reading is Leah Marcus's and the "lesbian" marriage reading is Philippa Berry's. See *Sodometries*, 36–43. See also Marcus, *Puzzling Shakespeare*, and Berry, *Of Chastity and Power*. For the use of *lesbian* in scare quotes or italics in reference to early modernity, see Traub, *The Renaissance of Lesbianism in Early Modern England*.

46 Goldberg, *Sodometries*, 58. The reference is to Kelly, "Did Women Have a Renaissance?"

47 For an exploration of the problem, in political theory, of women as citizens, on the one hand, and as sexual subjects, on the other, see, among others, Cora Kaplan's discussion of Mary Wollstonecraft in *Sea Changes*, especially chapter 2, 31–56. See also Freccero, "Notes of a Post–Sex Wars Theorizer."

48 The phrase "transformative articulation" is Butler's; see *Antigone's Claim*, 21.

5 *Queer Spectrality*

1 Derrida, *Specters of Marx*. The quotation comes from Derrida, "Marx and Sons," 254.

2 Derrida cites the phrase from *Hamlet*, "the time is out of joint" (3). *Specters* is, in part, a reading of *Hamlet*.

3 See *Specters of Marx*, 10; *Spectres de Marx*, 31.

4 Certeau, *L'écriture de l'histoire*, 8; *The Writing of History*, 2. Certeau is quoting Alphonse Dupront, "Langage et histoire."

5 Certeau, *Heterologies*, 8. Fredric Jameson makes the point that most ghosts are like those invoked by Certeau; "Derrida's ghosts . . . are not the truly malevolent ghosts of the modern tradition (perhaps in part because he is also willing to speak for them and to plead their cause) . . . ghosts, as we learned from Homer's land of the dead long ago, envy the living" ("Marx's Purloined Letter," 39).

6 For the "trauma of historicity," see Butler, "Burning Acts," and Freccero, "Historical Violence, Censorship, and the Serial Killer."

7 I do not wish to conflate the two terms *transsexual* and *transgender*, since their distinctions and their respective definitions are currently under debate, but I do want to signal that both were—perhaps still are—

emergent categories in movement and identity political discourse at around the same time. For some of the debates regarding the distinction between these terms, see Prosser, *Second Skins*, especially chapter 1. For an overview of some of the issues and problems in trans-discussions, see Halberstam, "Transgender Butch." I put "Brandon Teena" in scare quotes because part of what is at stake in the story is the way the proper name is linked to gender and also because the person in question used several proper names. As C. Jacob Hale notes, "Insistence on 'Brandon Teena' produces a representation of someone more solidly grounded in gendered social ontology than the subject (recon)figured by that name actually might have been" ("Consuming the Living," 314).

8 "Brandon Teena"'s rape and murder occurred in December 1993; the films and much of the commentary did not come until 1998, the same year that James Byrd and Matthew Shepard were killed. See Laplanche and Pontalis's discussion of "deferred action" in *The Language of Psychoanalysis*, 111–14.

9 What I mean here is that queer movement founds itself upon the crisis produced by the violent effacement of difference within a heteronormative social order. My use of the term *queer movement* follows bell hooks' argument for using the expression *feminist movement* without the definite article that defines it as one/a thing. See hooks, *Feminist Theory*. The story of Brandon Teena may be said to function in a manner akin to what Teresa de Lauretis calls a "public fantasy": "One might say that fantasy is the psychic mechanism that governs the translation of social representations into subjectivity and self-representation by a sort of adaptation or reworking of the social imaginary into individual fantasies. Let me then rephrase and say that sexuality is constructed or dynamically structured by fantasy in its various forms, conscious or unconscious, by daydreams and reveries as well as primal fantasies; to this list, which was Freud's, Laplanche has added a particular emphasis on parental fantasies, and I would also add public fantasies. . . . What I mean by public fantasies is dominant cultural narratives and scenarios of the popular imagination that have been expressed in myths, sacred texts, medieval sagas, Renaissance epics and their modern equivalents—novels, films, television, the internet, and so forth. As they contribute to the shaping of the social imaginary, public fantasies provide material and scripts, or forms of content and expression, to the subjective activity of fantasizing ("The Stubborn Drive," 865–66).

10 Hale, "Consuming the Living," 313.

11 See Halberstam, "Telling Tales," for a survey of these accounts.

12 Hale, "Consuming the Living," 318.

13 Spackman, "'Inter musam,'" 22. Spackman elaborates on the topos of the enchantress-turned-hag, noting that it is "a topos that opposes the beautiful enchantress (woman as lie) to the ugly, toothless old hag hidden beneath her artifice (woman as truth)."

14 Derrida, *Eperons/Spurs*, 102–5. This passage is cited in Spackman, "'Inter musam,'" 23n8.

15 Spackman, "'*Inter musam,*'" 23.

16 Hale, "Consuming the Living," 314.

17 Halberstam, "Telling Tales," 77.

18 Tom Kenworthy, "McKinney Avoids Death Sentence," *Washington Post*, November 5, 1999.

19 Popular culture beautifully and symptomatically captures this sense of haunting as a sign of trauma and the incompletion of the work of mourning. In a series of recent films, including *Ghost* (dir. Jerry Zucker, Paramount, 1990), *The Sixth Sense* (dir. M. Night Shyamalan, Hollywood Pictures/Spyglass Entertainment, 1999), *The Others* (dir. Alejandro Amenábar, Dimension Films/Cruise/Wagner Productions/Sogecine/Les Producciones del Escorpion, 2001), *Stir of Echoes* (dir. David Koepp, Artisan Entertainment/Hofflund/Polone Productions, 1999), and *The Ring* (dir. Gore Verbinski, Amblin Entertainment/BenderSpink/Dream Works SKG, 2002, based on the Japanese film *Ringu*, dir. Hideo Nakata, Kadokawa Shoten Publishing Co. Ltd./Omega Project, 1998), ghostly returns are accompanied by a demand that a traumatic event from the past be addressed and perhaps also "resolved." The returns, however, more often than not, figure the attachments, longings, and nonresolutions both of the ghosts themselves and of those whom they frequent. Further, in many cases, the ghosts do not even know that they are ghosts. Thus, part of the working through that allows them to recede involves their coming to terms with being "ghosted." See also, from an anthropological perspective, Rafael, *White Love and Other Events in Filippino History*.

20 Derrida, *Spectres de Marx*, 160; *Specters of Marx*, 97. As Wendy Brown points out, this notion of trauma and its injunctions counters a current logic she calls melancholic, which consists precisely in appealing to the law and to an economy of debt and repayment to effect a kind of closure in the present. She asks, "What anxiety about the way these past traumas live in the present might be signified by such impulses to re-

solve them through a discursive structure of wrong, debt, and payment?" *Politics out of History*, 140. See 170–71 for a related discussion of political melancholia.

21   See "Marx and Sons," 259, for Derrida's discussion of the difference between nostalgia and mourning in his discussion. There he also refers to "geopolitical mourning," the "paradoxical symptoms" of which he also understands *Specters of Marx* to be analyzing. In "Peines de mort," an interview with Elisabeth Roudinesco, Derrida also elaborates on the question of mourning and the distinction between incorporation and introjection (256–58).

22   Brown, *Politics out of History*, 150.

23   Castle, *The Apparitional Lesbian*, 2. Castle produces a kind of counterdiscourse from this effect, taking the spectrality seriously and turning it into a figure for the ways lesbianism makes its appearance in literary texts.

24   Derrida, *Spectres de Marx*, 165; *Specters of Marx*, 101.

25   Cixous, "The Laugh of the Medusa," 255.

26   Derrida, *Specters of Marx*, xviii, xix.

27   In "Marx's Purloined Letter," Jameson writes, "Mourning also wants to get rid of the past, to exorcize it, albeit under the guise of respectful commemoration. To forget the dead altogether is impious in ways that prepare their own retribution, but to remember the dead is neurotic and obsessive and merely feeds a sterile repetition. There is no 'proper' way of relating to the dead and the past" (58–59).

28   The expression "historical trauma" is Kaja Silverman's. In *Male Subjectivity at the Margins*, she writes, " 'historical trauma' may seem something of an oxymoron, since it uses an adjective connotative of the public sphere to qualify a noun conventionally associated with the psychic or physiological shock suffered by an individual person . . . By 'historical trauma' I mean a historically precipitated but psychoanalytically specific disruption, with ramifications extending far beyond the individual psyche" (55). She will go on, in the context of her study of male subjectivity, to argue its specificity as an effect in a group of men, but it seems to me equally applicable to the phenomena that Derrida and Gordon are describing, as well as to the sense of trauma conveyed in Cathy Caruth's *Unclaimed Experience*.

29   Gordon, *Ghostly Matters*, esp. 137–90.

30   For discussions of spectrality and materialism, see W. Brown, *Politics out of History*; also Jameson, "Marx's Purloined Letter," and Derrida's "Marx and Sons." See also Cheah, "Mattering."

31 Jameson uses the term *allegory* when clarifying his understanding of Derrida's discussion of class in *Specters of Marx*; "The point to be made, however, is not that all such class mappings are arbitrary and somehow subjective, but that they are inevitable allegorical grids through which we necessarily read the world" ("Marx's Purloined Letter," 49). Derrida remarks that he is unsure about the term ("Marx and Sons," 246). In *The Political Unconscious*, Jameson defines the allegorical: "The fullest form of what Althusser calls 'expressive causality' (and of what he calls 'historicism') will thus prove to be a vast interpretive allegory in which a sequence of historical events or texts and artifacts is rewritten in terms of some deeper, underlying, and more 'fundamental' narrative, of a hidden master narrative which is the allegorical key or figural content of the first sequence of empirical materials. This kind of allegorical master narrative would then include providential histories (such as those of Hegel or Marx), catastrophic visions of history (such as that of Spengler), and cyclical or Viconian visions of history alike. I read the Althusserian dictum, 'History is a process without a telos or a subject,' in this spirit, as a repudiation of such master narratives and their twin categories of narrative closure (telos) and of character (subject of history). As such historical allegories are also often characterized as being 'theological' " (28–29). For a discussion of the allegorical as it relates to ethnographic narrative, see Clifford, "On Ethnographic Allegory."

32 Fradenburg and Freccero, *Premodern Sexualities*, vii–xxiv.

33 Goldberg, "The History That Will Be."

34 A brief survey of New World and early modern colonial studies writing demonstrates the extent to which scholars are moved by an ethical imperative. To mention only a few whose framing of the ethical has prompted these musings: there is, of course, Todorov, *The Conquest of America*, originally published as *La conquête de l'Amérique*. Todorov makes his project an explicitly ethical one: "Mon intérêt principal est moins celui d'un historien que d'un moraliste" (12; "My main interest is less a historian's than a moralist's" [4]). But other examples might include Brandon, *New Worlds for Old*; Greenblatt, *Marvelous Possessions*; Certeau, *The Writing of History*; Hulme, *Colonial Encounters*; Pagden, *European Encounters with the New World*; Mignolo, *The Darker Side of the Renaissance*; and Goldberg, *Sodometries* and "The History That Will Be."

35 Pastor, "Silence and Writing"; White, *Metahistory* and "Historical Text as Literary Artifact." For the narration of desire, see de Lauretis, *Alice Doesn't*, especially "Desire in Narrative," 103–57.

36 Wolf, *Europe and the People without History*.

37   Carpentier, *The Lost Steps*, originally published as *Los pasos perdidos*.

38   With regard to the question of exemplarity, John Lyons makes the interesting point that in the case of Marguerite de Navarre's *Heptameron*, the woman's historical exemplarity is achieved precisely at the cost of a silencing of her voice. See *Exemplum*, 72–117. Note the degree to which this is true of female historical and literary figures, such as Lucretia, whose rape and death launch her into historical significance as exemplary originator of Republican Rome. See Jed, *Chaste Thinking*.

39   Gubar, " 'The Blank Page' and the Issues of Female Creativity." For an interesting feminist consideration of the interplay between voice, silence, and writing that also, tellingly, begins with a story of a woman, Philomela, whose tongue is removed, see Joplin, "The Voice of the Shuttle Is Ours," 35–64.

40   Pastor cites Cortés's comment about "la lengua que yo tengo, que es una india de esta tierra" (148; the tongue that I have, who is an Indian woman from this land); see also Cortés, *Cartas de relación*, 44. In *The Conquest of America*, Todorov cites Bernal Díaz as reporting that the nickname given to Cortés was that of Malinche (101). See also Díaz, *Historia verdadera de la conquista de México* and *The Conquest of New Spain*. Greenblatt, in *Marvelous Possessions*, also discusses this text and the question of Doña Marina's relation to Cortés in chapter 5, "The Go-Between," 128–46.

41   Ovid, *Metamorphoses*, book III, ll. 339–510 (148–61). Much has been written in a feminist vein regarding the story of Echo and Narcissus; see in particular, Spivak, "Echo," in *The Spivak Reader*; also Enterline, *The Rhetoric of the Body from Ovid to Shakespeare*. Spivak makes the point that Echo does, nevertheless, speak her desire through a strategy of mimicry, whereby only parts of Narcissus's sentences are in fact echoed, the parts that could be said to constitute her desire.

42   Greenblatt, *Marvelous Possessions*, 11–12.

43   Todorov, *The Conquest of America*, 4.

44   Todorov, like Pastor, also invokes another figure of loss that is gendered: "Une femme maya est morte dévorée par les chiens. . . . J'écris ce livre pour essayer de faire en sorte qu'on n'oublie pas ce récit, et mille autres pareils" (306–7; "A Mayan woman died, devoured by dogs. . . . I am writing this book to prevent this story and a thousand others like it from being forgotten" [246–47]). He dedicates the book, in fact, to her memory. The difference between Pastor's women's voices and the inert mute body of the disappeared Mayan woman in Todorov's text highlights one of the differences between a guilty, reparative project of com-

memoration and a project of feminist recovery in which identification plays a role.

45 Goldberg, "The History That Will Be," 17. Goldberg is commenting on an essay by Stephen Greenblatt, "Invisible Bullets."

46 Derrida, "Archive Fever," 27. See also the later, slightly expanded version, *Archive Fever*, originally published as *Mal d'archive*. He is referring here to Walter Benjamin's concept of "messianic" time; see "Theses on the Philosophy of History," 253–64.

47 In "Peines de mort," Derrida begins to make distinctions among the various terms for *ghost*, *spectre* (including also *fantasme* and *fantôme*) implying a certain relation to visibility on the one hand, and *revenant*, which, through its disconnection with regimes of visibility, registers the unforeseeability of the event, on the other (256n1). However, in *Specters of Marx*, it seems to me, there is an oscillation between the two that I wish to exploit, since the returning ghosts in question here both invoke the possibility of vision and simultaneously elude visual (and scribal) mastery.

48 Jameson, "Marx's Purloined Letter," 44. Jameson invokes both queer theory and mestizo "intellectual politics" in this context (45). Another way he poses the question of the "unmixed" as conceptual target is to say "a world cleansed of spectrality is precisely ontology itself, a world of pure essence, of immediate density, of things without a past" (58). See also Derrida, *Specters of Marx*.

49 W. Brown, *Politics out of History*, 149–50.

50 Gordon, *Ghostly Matters*, 179. Later on in the book she writes, "Haunting is the sociality of living with ghosts" (201).

51 Abraham and Torok, *The Shell and the Kernel*, 1:172; the work was originally published as *L'écorce et le noyau*. In "Fors," Derrida's preface to Abraham and Torok's *Cryptonymie*, Derrida makes a distinction between the "foreigner incorporated in the crypt of the Self," as the psychic phenomenon that Abraham and Torok analyze in relation to mourning and melancholia, and the sense of haunting as a collective and historical effect:

Bien que les mots 'fantôme' ou 'hantise' s'imposent parfois pour désigner les habitants de la crypte à l'intérieur du Moi (morts vivant comme 'des corps étrangers dans le subject'), il faut rigoureusement distinguer l'étranger incorporé dans la crypte du Moi et le fantôme qui vient hanter depuis l'Inconscient d'un autre. Le fantôme a son lieu dans l'Inconscient, lui, et il n'est pas l'effet d'un refoulement 'proper' au sujet

qu'il vient hanter avec toute sorte de ventriloquies, mais 'proper' à un
inconscient parental. La revenance n'est pas un retour du refoulé . . . il
s'agit d'un secret, d'une tombe et d'un enterrement, mais la crypte d'où
revient le fantôme est celle d'un autre. (42n1)

Although the words 'ghost' [*fantôme*] or 'haunting' are sometimes un-
avoidable in designating the inhabitants of the crypt within the Self (the
living dead as 'foreign bodies in the subject'), one must rigorously distinguish between the foreigner incorporated in the crypt of the Self and
the ghost that comes haunting out of the Unconscious of the other. The
ghost does have a place in the Unconscious; but he is not an effect of
repression 'belonging' to the subject he comes to haunt with all kinds of
ventriloquism; he is rather 'proper' to a parental unconscious. Coming
back to haunt [*la revenance*] is not a return of the repressed . . . What is
in question in both is a secret, a tomb, and a burial, but the crypt from
which the ghost comes back belongs to someone else. (Abraham and
Torok, *The Wolf Man's Magic Word*, 119n21)

As Gordon puts it, "the ghost cannot be simply tracked back to an individual loss or trauma. The ghost has its own desires, so to speak, which
figure the whole complicated sociality of a determining formation" (183).

52 W. Brown, *Politics out of History*, 146.

53 For various accounts of the ghost dance, see, among others,
D. Brown, *Bury My Heart at Wounded Knee*; Debo, *A History of the Indians
of the United States*; and Mooney, *The Ghost-Dance Religion and the Sioux
Outbreak of 1890*. See also Roach, *Cities of the Dead*, 202–11. Roach, however, considers the ghost dance a "rite of memory" (208), and it is unclear
therefore whether he sees the dance as commemorative or performative. He
also views it as an act of self-possession—and thus potentially identitarian in its aspirations—whereas in my argument and in Spivak's, the
ghost dance would be rather an opening onto inhabitation by others.

54 Spivak, "Ghostwriting," 70.

55 Derrida, "Fors," xvii ("La crypte est le caveau d'un désir" [*Cryptonymie*, 18]).

56 Abraham, *The Shell and the Kernel*, 188.

57 How might this willingness to be haunted by desire serve justice,
not only for the past, but for the present and the future too? Derrida's
exhortation suggests that "[Il faut] parler du fantôme, voire au fantôme
et avec lui, [dès lors qu'] aucune éthique, aucune politique, révolutionnaire ou non, ne paraît possible et pensable et juste, qui ne reconnaisse
à son principe le respect pour ces autres qui ne sont plus ou pour ces

autres qui ne sont pas encore là, présentement vivants, qu'ils soient déjà morts ou qu'ils ne soient pas encore nés" (*Spectres de Marx*, 15; "To speak of the ghost, indeed to the ghost and with it, . . . no ethics, no politics, whether revolutionary nor not, seems possible and thinkable and just that does not recognize in its principle the respect for those others who are no longer or for those others who are not yet there, presently living, whether they are already dead or not yet born" [*Specters of Marx*, xix]).

58 "Historiography as hauntology is thus more than a new mode of figuring the presence of the past, the ineffable and unconquerable force of the past; it also opens the stage for battling with the past over possibilities for the future" (Brown, *Politics out of History*, 151).

59 I put the word *colonial* in quotation marks to signal the complex and ambiguous role Jean de Léry and France itself could be said to have played in relation to early modern colonialism in the New World. France did not have "colonies," strictly speaking, in Brazil, and Léry's religious mission did not explicitly include indigenous conversion.

60 Nakam, *Au lendemain de la Saint-Barthélemy*.

61 Léry, *Histoire d'un voyage*, facsimile edition. See also the edition edited by Frank Lestringant. All citations refer to the Lestringant edition, except as otherwise noted. I use Janet Whatley's English translation.

62 The evidence testifying to the persistence of Saint-Barthélemy as traumatic national memory includes, among other things, the film *La reine Margot* (dir. Patrice Chéreau, Miramax/Renn/France 2 Cinema/ D.A. Films, 1994), which links that massacre obscurely to the AIDS epidemic, as well as numerous national commemorations that occur annually in Paris itself. See Renan, "Qu'est-ce qu'une nation?" 892: "Tout citoyen français doit avoir oublié la Saint-Barthélemy." The injunction to forget is in part what reveals the traumatic force of the event. Renan's comment is cited in Anderson, *Imagined Communities*. I thank Sharon Kinoshita for directing me to this reference. I use the term *modern* here not because I think it is necessarily a modern massacre, but because, coming as it does near the end of the century of religious wars and just before the peace Henri IV will briefly bring to France, it is a traumatic event seen to precede France's "modern"—and nationalist—accession to secularism.

63 I have written about this aspect of cannibalism elsewhere; see "Cannibalism, Homophobia, Women"; and, more recently, "Early Modern Psychoanalytics." On the relation between cannibalism and historiographic practice, see Freccero, "Toward a Psychoanalytics of Historiography."

64 Derrida, "Peines de mort," 257–58; my translation.

65 See the fascinating collection of essays that approaches the topic from both psychoanalytic and anthropological perspectives in *Destins du cannibalisme*, a 1972 special issue of the *Nouvelle revue de psychanalyse*.

66 Léry also discusses Sancerre in a chapter significantly enlarged in the 1599 edition of the *Histoire*, appended as chapter 15 bis in the Lestringant edition. This enlarged chapter is especially interesting, as the editor notes, for being an "essai flamboyant de comparatisme cannibale" (42), and it includes xenophobic diatribes against the Turks and the Italians. Nevertheless, the culmination of the diatribe targets France as most ferocious and extravagant in its cannibalistic excesses. See 571–95.

67 See chapter 18 for Léry's account of the first night he spends in a Tupi village where, during a drunken celebration, he is offered "a foot" to eat by one of the villagers. Not understanding the language, Léry fears that he will be eaten next; in the morning he learns his error through his interpreter and concludes the account thus: "Après qu'il eut le tout recité aux sauvages, lesquels s'esjouyssans de ma venue, me pensans caresser, n'avoyent bougé d'aupres de moy toute la nuict: eux ayans dit qu'ils s'estoyent aussi aucunement apperceus que j'avois eu peur d'eux, dont ils estoyent bien marris, ma consolation fut (selon qu'ils sont grands gausseurs) une risée qu'ils firent, de ce que sans y penser, ils me l'avoyent baillée si belle" (453; "When he recounted the whole business to the savages—who, rejoicing at my coming, and thinking to show me affection, had not budged from my side all night—they said that they had sensed that I had been somewhat frightened of them, for which they were very sorry. My one consolation was the hoot of laughter they sent up—for they are great jokers—at having [without meaning to] given me such a scare" [163–64]).

68 Lestringant, *Le cannibale*, 145–57; *Cannibals*, 82–84. See also Gaignebet, *Le coeur mangé*. Boccaccio's fourth and fifth days also feature adaptations of the European motif of revenge cannibalism or "love-vengeance." See also Lupton, "Secularization and Its Symptoms."

69 For a discussion of Montaigne's use of the metaphor of cannibalism to describe the French wars of religion, see Quint, "A Reconsideration of Montaigne's 'Des Cannibales.'" Many sixteenth-century Protestants also made the comparison between New World cannibalism and Catholicism. For a modern discussion of the relation between the two, see, among others, Hulme, *Colonial Encounters*; also Kilgour, *From Communion to Cannibalism*; and Barker, Hulme, and Iversen, *Cannibalism and the Colonial World*.

70 Las Casas, *The Devastation of the Indies*; see also *Brevísima relación de la destruición de las Indias*. Dogs appear frequently in Las Casas's text as one of the primary weapons of the Spanish and act as proxy cannibals, dismembering and devouring the Indians.

71 "Mais afin de renvoyer l'horrible cruauté en l'Amerique mesme, non pas seulement exercé par les naturels habitans les uns contre les autres, mais beaucoup plus detestablement par les Espagnols sur les miserables nations de ces païs-là, lesquelles Dieu par son juste jugement a livrées entre leurs mains, il faut voir le livre de frere Barthelemi de las Casas" (*Histoire d'un voyage*, 591; But, in order to return this horrible cruelty to America itself, not only the cruelty exercised by the natural inhabitants each against the other, but much more detestably by the Spanish against the miserable nations of that country, one must consult the book by brother Barthelemy de las Casas [my translation]). See also Montaigne, *Oeuvres complètes*, book III, chapter 6, 876–93.

72 La Boétie, *Discours de la servitude volontaire*, 171. The editor notes that the term is also used to describe certain kings in Homer's *Iliad*. For an extended discussion of this treatise and Etienne de La Boétie's political and literary significance, see Schachter, *"Voluntary Servitude" and the Politics of Friendship*. I thank Marc for drawing this expression to my attention.

73 For discussions of the idealizing exoticization—and temporal fixing—of what is (also) considered primitive, see Diamond, *In Search of the Primitive*; Fabian, *Time and the Other*; Rosaldo, "The Use and Abuse of Anthropology"; Clifford, "On Ethnographic Allegory"; and McClintock, *Imperial Leather*. Léry, however, does not engage in the "critical nostalgia" Clifford analyzes as the classic ethnographic gesture that both ascribes to the indigenous other an authenticity felt to have been lost and produces the other as disappearing, preserved only in the text of the ethnographer. In fact, Montaigne's "ethnographic allegory" in "Des cannibales" much more closely resembles the topoi Clifford examines than does Léry's account, which does not posit the Tupinamba as a society-in-disappearance. See Montaigne, *Oeuvres complètes*, book I, chapter 31.

74 For an analysis of the homoerotics of Léry's description in this chapter, see Neuber, "Jean de Léry's Queer Identifications."

75 Goldberg observes a similar phenomenon of the destabilization of both racial and gender identity in relation to Cabeza de Vaca in *Sodometries*, 210–16. He writes, "Cabeza de Vaca's fractured and divided identity is striated by oppositions that it never fully inhabits. The axes of identification and difference are not separated by the normative Spanish/Indian

opposition; nor is the absoluteness of gender difference, which Cabeza de Vaca seems to endorse as he writes his ethnographies, borne on his naked and burdened body" (213–14).

76 R. Greene, *Unrequited Conquests*, 77–134. See also Raffles, *In Amazonia.*

77 See my discussion of Petrarch's canzone 23 in "Ovidian Subjectivities in Early Modern Lyric."

78 The Lestringant edition includes a fascinating footnote (403n1) to this passage pointing out that Claude Lévi-Strauss, in *Tristes tropiques*— the account of a trip explicitly undertaken following in the footsteps of Léry's work, which Lévi-Strauss refers to as the "premier modèle d'une monographie d'ethnologue" (8)—also refers to the "joy" and "ravishment" of the music he hears when he encounters the Bororo.

79 See the footnote to this passage, 508n2. Lestringant points out that this seems a revolutionary thing to say in travel literature of the sixteenth century; he qualifies it by saying that it should be understood in the context of an intent to condemn the homeland rather than praise the "natives." He also notes here that the myth of the Noble Savage is not yet in existence: "Le Bon Sauvage des Lumières sortira nu et radieux de ce regard mélancholique jeté une dernière fois par le voyageur en partance pour l'Europe."

80 Goldberg, *Sodometries*, 179–222.

81 See also Bray, *Homosexuality in Renaissance England.*

82 Goldberg's description of preposterous logic applies uncannily to the deployment of sodomitical rhetoric subsequent to the events of September 11, 2001; see my " 'They Are All Sodomites!' " In *Homos*, Bersani provocatively argues that "Male heterosexuality would be a *traumatic* privileging of difference" (39). In "Is the Rectum a Grave?" he notes that the gesture to overcome identification—"a fearful male response to the seductiveness of an image of sexual powerlessness"—in fact encourages, if not produces, the violent effacement Goldberg analyzes. Thus Bersani argues, "the most brutal machismo is really part of a domesticating, even sanitizing project" (221).

83 See my "Heteroerotic Homoeroticism."

84 The term *displaced abjection* is Jonathan Dollimore's; see *Sexual Dissidence*. See also Traub, *The Renaissance of Lesbianism in Early Modern England*: "The history of perversion often involves a displaced abjection whereby that which is marginalized in fact originates in that which has the power to repudiate. . . . abjection can be rooted as much in a terror (and disavowal) of *similarity* as of difference. It is not just fear of the diametri-

cally opposed other, but anxiety about the proximate, the adjacent, the familiar, that can initiate the historical mechanisms of perversion" (258).

85 Greenblatt writes about this episode at length in *Marvelous Possessions*, 14–19, focusing on the movement from revulsion to wonder Léry experiences in the course of witnessing the ceremony. See also Certeau, *L'écriture de l'histoire*, 238–41; *The Writing of History*, 209–43; and Freccero, "Heteroerotic Homoeroticism."

86 Freud, "Some Psychological Consequences of the Anatomical Distinction Between the Sexes"; *Standard Edition of the Complete Psychological Works of Sigmund Freud*, 248–58. See also Freud's discussion of the case of the Wolf Man, "From the History of an Infantile Neurosis." As Silverman writes in *Male Subjectivity at the Margins*, "the spectacle of the primal scene encourages identifications which are in excess of sexual difference . . . it promotes, in other words, desire for the father and identification with the mother, as well as desire for the mother and identification with the father. In addition, it disposes of anatomical lack in ways that are profoundly disruptive of conventional masculinity" (165). She will go on to define this conjunction of masculine-masculine identification and desire as "sodomitical identification" (173). For an assessment of the overall significance of the primal scene, see Laplanche and Pontalis, *Vocabulaire de la psychanalyse*, 432: "Freud met en lumière sur ce cas différents éléments: le coït est compris par l'enfant comme une agression du père dans une relation sado-masochique; il provoque une excitation sexuelle chez l'enfant en même temps qu'il fournit un support à l'angoisse de castration; il est interprété dans le cadre d'une théorie sexuelle infantile comme coït anal" ("Freud brings out different aspects: first, the act of coitus is understood by the child as an aggression by the father in a sado-masochistic relationship; secondly, the scene gives rise to sexual excitation in the child while at the same time providing a basis for castration anxiety; thirdly, the child interprets what is going on, within the framework of an infantile sexual theory, as anal coitus," *The Language of Psychoanalysis* [335]).

87 Bersani writes: "I call jouissance 'self-shattering' in that it disrupts the ego's coherence and dissolves its boundaries. . . . self-shattering is intrinsic to the homo-ness in homosexuality. Homo-ness is an anti-identitarian identity" (*Homos*, 101). In a long and careful argument that spans several essays and books, Bersani outlines his theory of the willingness to sacrifice or relinquish control for the sake of pleasure that he regards as one of the potentially distinctive features of male homoerotic subjectivity. See "Is the Rectum a Grave?", *Homos*, and "Sociality and Sexuality." In *Homos*, Bersani also reinterprets the Wolf Man's dream

(108–12) to demonstrate Freud's investment in castration anxiety at the expense of what Bersani reads as "one genealogy of gay love": "We might imagine that a man being fucked is generously offering the sight of his own penis as a gift or even a replacement for what is temporarily being 'lost' inside him—an offering not made in order to calm his partner's fears of castration but rather as the gratuitous and therefore even lovelier protectiveness that all human beings need when they take the risk of merging with another, of risking their own boundaries for the sake of self-dissolving extensions" (112).

88 Silverman, *Male Subjectivity at the Margins*, 173.

89 Cheng, *The Melancholy of Race*, xi.

90 See also Sollors, *Beyond Ethnicity*.

91 Hope, "Melancholic Modernity." See also Freccero, "Early Modern Psychoanalytics."

92 Derrida wants to make a distinction between the ghost in Abraham and Torok's crypt of the self and "the ghost that comes haunting out of the Unconscious of the other" ("Fors," 42n1; *The Wolf Man's Magic Word*, 119n21)—in other words, between the ghost that comes from elsewhere and the one that comes from the subject's own unconscious. Cheng and Butler, I think, theorize a way for the ghost to be from/in both places at once.

93 Butler writes in *The Psychic Life of Power*: "The psychic form of reflexivity melancholia elaborates carries the trace of the other within it as a dissimulated sociality . . . The melancholic does not merely withdraw the lost object from consciousness, but withdraws into the psyche a configuration of the social world as well" (181).

94 "Melancholia appears to be a process of internalization, and one might well read its effects as a psychic state that has effectively substituted itself for the world in which it dwells" (ibid., 179). The use of the word *fictional* here derives from Lacan; see Butler, *The Psychic Life of Power*, 196. Slavoj Žižek has written a diagnostic critique of the recent critical privileging of melancholia over mourning in Freud's theory of loss as an error of political correctness. He asserts that "The melancholic link to the lost ethnic Object allows us to claim that we remain faithful to our ethnic roots while fully participating in the global capitalist game" ("Melancholy and the Act," 659). I understand Cheng and Butler to be using melancholia as a diagnostic tool in part for understanding the phenomenon Žižek identifies and thus not to be committing the error he is denouncing.

95 See Muñoz, *Disidentifications*, for a discussion of the complexities

of identification for minoritarian subjects. Paraphrasing and extending Sedgwick's discussion of identification in *Epistemology of the Closet*, Muñoz writes, "Identifying with an object, person, lifestyle, history, political ideology, religious orientation, and so on, means also simultaneously and partially counteridentifying, as well as only partially identifying, with different aspects of the social and psychic world" (8). Although in the introduction he seems to describe "disidentification" as a liability of identification, he later reworks the term to demonstrate how it enables alternative modes of subjectivity and relationality. He also discusses melancholia in a chapter about Van DerZee's *The Harlem Book of the Dead*, Isaac Julien's *Looking for Langston*, and the photography of Robert Mapplethorpe. He wants to argue for a depathologizing of melancholia in order to understand it "as a 'structure of feeling' that is necessary and not always counterproductive and negative. I am proposing that melancholia, for blacks, queers, or any queers of color, is not a pathology but an integral part of everyday lives" (74). This is something Cheng is also attempting to address without, however, wanting, as does Muñoz, to redeem melancholia.

96 See Georges Van Den Abbeele's introduction to his *Travel as Metaphor from Montaigne to Rousseau*, where he explores the topoi of travel narratives (and narrative as travel) that work both as containment strategies and as modes of unexpected and unpredictable estrangement: "It should be acknowledged," he writes, "that the voyage . . . has a powerful ability to dislodge the framework in which it is placed or understood, to subject it to critical displacement—although that displacement is not always to where one expects, nor is its criticism necessarily what one expects to find. The voyage, in other words, always takes us somewhere" (xxx). In an interesting discussion of home or *oikos* as a "privileged point" of fixity and return that is nevertheless "posited *après coup*," after the voyage has begun, he helps clarify some of the ways in which the voyage itself changes or transforms the "homeland" for the traveler. He also points out that, in the tradition, a gendered topography obtains (most famously articulated through the voyage of Ulysses) whereby "the unpredictable pleasure/anxiety of travel" is couched "in terms of a male eros both attracted and repulsed by sexual difference" (xxv) and thus that travel enacts an allegory of (hetero)sexual difference. Here too, it seems to me, Léry differs, in that the allegory inscribed is less oedipal than "reverse oedipal"; not a filial-paternal agon enacted across the landscape of the mother's body, but an intramasculine merging instead. This brings Léry's voyage closer to those later, explicitly "homosexual," voyages that stage

an encounter with racial difference, such as found in Oscar Wilde, André
Gide, Roland Barthes, and Jean Genet; see Dollimore, *Sexual Dissidence*.

97 Clifford, "On Ethnographic Allegory," 112.

98 Derrida, *Specters of Marx*, 101 ("une structure d'apparition disparais-
sante" [*Spectres de Marx*, 165]).

99 J. Greene, "New Historicism and Its New World Discoveries,"
193n32. See, for the account of this court proceeding, D'Avezac, *Campagne du navire l'Espoir de Honfleur*, 12–13. D'Avezac tells the story to explain how Gonneville's travel narrative came to be discovered and subsequently published. It was submitted as evidence in the court case by
the descendants of Gonneville and Essomeric, the Tupi boy who traveled
from Brazil to France with Gonneville.

100 Greene, "New Historicism," 176; D'Avezac, *Campagne du navire
l'Espoir de Honfleur*, 101–2.

101 W. Brown, *Politics out of History*, 140.

102 Derrida, *Spectres de Marx*, 160; *Specters of Marx*, 97.

103 I am not suggesting that Léry was anywhere near where Essomeric and his family were to be found, but rather that his musing that
he seems to have them before his eyes "even now" (twenty years after
the fact, and in France) does not describe a far-fetched impossibility.
Of course, the question of visibility is also at issue here, since the spectral brings into play what Derrida calls "la *fréquence* d'une certaine visibilité. Mais la visibilité de l'invisible. Et la visibili*té*, par essence, ne se
voit pas. . . . le spectre, c'est aussi, entre autres choses, ce qu'on imagine,
ce qu'on croit voir et qu'on projette" (*Spectres de Marx*, 165; "the *frequency*
of a certain visibility. But the visibility of the invisible. And visibili*ty*, by
its essence, is not seen. . . . The specter is also, among other things, what
one imagines, what one thinks one sees and which one projects" [*Specters
of Marx*, 100–101]).

104 Derrida urges us to "exorcise" ghosts, but, as he says, "Exorciser
non pas pour chasser les fantômes, mais cette fois pour leur faire droit,
si cela revient à les faire revenir vivants, comme des revenants qui ne
seraient plus des revenants, mais comme ces autres arrivants auxquels une
mémoire ou une promesse hospitalière doit donner accueil—sans la cer-
titude, jamais, qu'ils se présentent comme tels. Non pour leur faire droit
en ce sens mais par souci de *justice*" (*Spectres de Marx*, 277–78; "not in
order to chase away the ghosts, but this time to grant them the right,
if it means making them come back alive, as *revenants* who would no
longer be *revenants*, but as other *arrivants* to whom a hospitable memory or promise must offer welcome—without certainty, ever, that they

present themselves as such. Not in order to grant them the right in this sense but out of a concern for *justice*" [*Specters of Marx*, 175]).

105 Benjamin, "Theses on the Philosophy of History," 257–58, IX. Wendy Brown, in *Politics out of History*, notes that the angel is paralyzed and helpless and that it is therefore incumbent upon us to seize the moment, to interrupt the storm (155–62). She describes Benjamin's understanding of the agents of this process in what seem to me to be humanist terms, in that we are indeed the agents of history who do the interrupting. In using this image, I want first to suspend the definition of the storm, which in Benjamin's text is "what we call progress," and also, if possible, to suspend the question of agency within the image. What, after all, we might ask, is an angel?

Bibliography

Abraham, Nicolas, and Maria Torok. *Cryptonymie: Le verbier de l'Homme aux loups*. Paris: Aubier Flammarion, 1976.

————. *The Wolf Man's Magic Word: A Cryptonymy*. Translated by Nicholas Rand. Minneapolis: University of Minnesota Press, 1986.

————. *L'écorce et le noyau*. Paris: Flammarion, 1987.

————. *The Shell and the Kernel: Renewals of Psychoanalysis*. Edited and translated by Nicholas Rand. Chicago: University of Chicago Press, 1994.

Aers, David. "A Whisper in the Ear of Early Modernists; or, Reflections on Literary Critics Writing the 'History of the Subject.'" In *Culture and History 1350–1600: Essays on English Communities, Identities and Writing*, edited by David Aers, 177–202. London: Harvester, 1992.

Althusser, Louis. "Ideology and Ideological State Apparatuses (Notes toward an Investigation)." In *Lenin and Philosophy, and Other Essays by Louis Althusser*, edited and translated by Ben Brewster. New York: Monthly Review Press, 1971.

Altman, Dennis. "Global Gaze/Global Gays." *GLQ: A Journal of Lesbian and Gay Studies* 3 (1997): 417–36.

Anderson, Benedict. *Imagined Communities: Reflections on the Origin and Spread of Nationalism*. 1983. Reprint, London: Verso, 1987.

Apuleius. *Metamorphosis*. Volume 2. Edited and translated by J. Arthur Hanson. Cambridge, Mass.: Harvard University Press, 1989.

Archibald, Elizabeth. *Incest and the Medieval Imagination*. Oxford: Clarendon, 2001.

Ascoli, Albert. "Pyrrhus' Rules: Playing with Power from Boccaccio to Machiavelli." *MLN* 114 (1999): 14–57.

Audi, Robert. *The Cambridge Dictionary of Philosophy*. 2nd ed. Cambridge: Cambridge University Press, 1995.

Baker, Houston. "In Dubious Battle." *New Literary History* 18.2 (1987): 363–69.

Balakrishnan, Gopal, ed. *Mapping the Nation*. London: Verso, 1996.

Barker, Francis, Peter Hulme, and Margaret Iverson, eds. *Cannibalism and the Colonial World*. Cambridge: Cambridge University Press, 1998.

Barthes, Roland. *Fragments d'un discours amoureux*. Paris: Editions du Seuil, 1977.

———. *A Lover's Discourse: Fragments*. Translated by Richard Howard. New York: Hill and Wang, 1978.

Benjamin, Walter. "Theses on the Philosophy of History." In *Illuminations: Essays and Reflections*, edited by Hannah Arendt, translated by Harry Zohn, 253–64. New York: Schocken Books, 1969.

Berlant, Lauren. *The Queen of America Goes to Washington City: Essays on Sex and Citizenship*. Durham, N.C.: Duke University Press, 1997.

———. ed. *Intimacy*. Chicago: University of Chicago Press, 2001.

Berlant, Lauren, and Elizabeth Freeman. "Queer Nationality." In *Fear of a Queer Planet: Queer Politics and Social Theory*, edited by Michael Warner, 193–229. Minneapolis: University of Minnesota Press, 1993.

Berlant, Lauren, and Michael Warner. "What Does Queer Theory Teach Us about X?" *PMLA* 110 (1995): 343–49.

Bernheimer, Charles, ed. *Comparative Literature in the Age of Multiculturalism*. Baltimore: Johns Hopkins University Press, 1995.

Berry, Philippa. *Of Chastity and Power: Elizabethan Literature and the Unmarried Queen*. London: Routledge, 1989.

Bersani, Leo. "Is the Rectum a Grave?" *October* 43 (1987): 197–222.

———. *Homos*. Cambridge, Mass.: Harvard University Press, 1995.

———. "Sociality and Sexuality." *Critical Inquiry* 26.4 (2000): 641–56.

Bhabha, Homi. "DissemiNation." In *The Location of Culture*, 139–70. London: Routledge, 1994.

Boccaccio, Giovanni. *Decameron*. Edited by Vittore Branca. Florence: Felice Le Monnier, 1960.

———. *The Decameron*. Translated by John Payne, revised by Charles Singleton. Berkeley: University of California Press, 1982.

Boehrer, Bruce Thomas. *Monarchy and Incest in Renaissance England: Literature, Culture, Kinship, and Kingship*. Philadelphia: University of Pennsylvania Press, 1992.

Borneman, John. "Until Death Do Us Part: Marriage/Death in Anthropological Discourse." *American Ethnologist* 23.2 (1996): 215–38.

Borrillo, Daniel, Eric Fassin, and Marcela Jacub, eds. *Au-delà du* PACS: *L'expertise familiale à l'épreuve de l'homosexualité*. Paris: Presses Universitaires de France, 1999.

Boswell, John. *Christianity, Social Tolerance, and Homosexuality: Gay People in Western Europe from the Beginning of the Christian Era to the Fourteenth Century*. Chicago: University of Chicago Press, 1980.

———. *Same-Sex Unions in Premodern Europe*. New York: Vintage, 1994.

Braidotti, Rosi. "Envy; or With Your Brains and My Looks." In *Men in Feminism*, edited by Alice Jardine and Paul Smith, 233–41. New York: Routledge, 1989.

———. *Patterns of Dissonance*. Oxford: Polity, 1991.

———. *Nomadic Subjects: Embodiment and Sexual Difference in Contemporary Feminist Theory*. New York: Columbia University Press, 1994.

Brandon, William. *New Worlds for Old: Reports from the New World and their Effect on the Development of Social Thought in Europe, 1500–1800*. Athens: Ohio University Press, 1986.

Bray, Alan. *Homosexuality in Renaissance England*. New York: Columbia University Press, 1995.

Brown, Dee. *Bury My Heart at Wounded Knee: An Indian History of the American West*. 1970. Reprint, New York: Pocket Books, 1981.

Brown, Marshall, ed. *Periodization: Cutting Up the Past*. Special issue. *Modern Language Quarterly* 62.4 (2001).

Brown, Wendy. *States of Injury: Power and Freedom in Late Modernity*. Princeton, N.J.: Princeton University Press, 1995.

———. "The Impossibility of Women's Studies." *Differences: A Journal of Feminist Cultural Studies* 9.3 (1997): 79–101.

———. *Politics out of History*. Princeton, N.J.: Princeton University Press, 2001.

Brucker, Gene, ed. *The Society of Renaissance Florence: A Documentary Study*. New York: Harper and Row, 1971.

Butler, Judith. *Gender Trouble: Feminism and the Subversion of Identity*. New York: Routledge, 1990.

———. "Imitation and Gender Insubordination." In *Inside/Out: Lesbian Theories, Gay Theories*, edited by Diana Fuss, 13–31. New York: Routledge, 1991.

———. "Contingent Foundations: Feminism and the Question of 'Postmodernism.'" In *Feminists Theorize the Political*, edited by Judith Butler and Joan Scott, 3–21. New York: Routledge, 1992.

———. *Bodies That Matter: On the Discursive Limits of "Sex."* New York: Routledge, 1993.

————. "Critically Queer." *GLQ: A Journal of Lesbian and Gay Studies* 1 (1993): 17–32.

————. "Against Proper Objects." *Differences: A Journal of Feminist Cultural Studies* 6.2–3 (1994): 1–26.

————. "Burning Acts: Injurious Speech." In *Deconstruction Is/in America: A New Sense of the Political*, edited by Anselm Haverkamp, 149–80. New York: New York University Press, 1995.

————. *The Psychic Life of Power: Theories in Subjection.* Stanford, Calif.: Stanford University Press, 1997.

————. "Merely Cultural." *Social Text* 52/53 (1997): 265–77.

————. *Antigone's Claim: Kinship between Life and Death.* New York: Columbia University Press, 2000.

Carpentier, Alejo. *Los pasos perdidos.* Edited by Roberto González Echevarría. Madrid: Cátedra, 1985.

————. *The Lost Steps.* Translated by Harriet de Onís. Minneapolis: University of Minnesota Press, 2001.

Caruth, Cathy. *Unclaimed Experience: Trauma, Narrative, and History.* Baltimore: Johns Hopkins University Press, 1996.

Case, Sue-Ellen. "Tracking the Vampire." *Differences: A Journal of Feminist Cultural Studies* 3.2 (1991): 1–20.

Castle, Terry. *The Apparitional Lesbian: Female Homosexuality and Modern Culture.* New York: Columbia University Press, 1993.

Cave, Terence. *The Cornucopian Text: Problems of Writing in the French Renaissance.* Oxford: Clarendon, 1979.

Cazauran, Nicole. "La trentième nouvelle de l'*Heptaméron* ou la méditation d'un 'exemple.' " In *Mélanges de littérature du moyen âge au XXe siècle offerts à Mlle. Jeanne Lods*, 617–52. Paris: Ecole normale supérieure de jeunes filles, 1978.

Certeau, Michel de. *L'écriture de l'histoire.* Paris: Gallimard, 1975.

————. *Heterologies: Discourse on the Other.* Translated by Brian Massumi. Minneapolis: University of Minnesota Press, 1986.

————. *The Writing of History.* Translated by Tom Conley. New York: Columbia University Press, 1988.

Chakrabarty, Dipesh. *Provincializing Europe: Postcolonial Thought and Historical Difference.* Princeton, N.J.: Princeton University Press, 2000.

Cheah, Pheng. "Mattering." *Diacritics* 26.1 (1996): 108–39.

Cheng, Anne Anlin. *The Melancholy of Race: Psychoanalysis, Assimilation, and Hidden Grief.* New York: Oxford University Press, 2001.

Christian, Barbara. "The Race for Theory." *Cultural Critique* 6 (1987): 51–63.

Cixous, Hélène. "The Laugh of the Medusa." In *New French Feminisms: An Anthology*, edited by Elaine Marks and Isabelle de Courtivron, 245–64. New York: Schocken Books, 1981.

Clifford, James. "On Ethnographic Allegory." In *Writing Culture: The Poetics and Politics of Ethnography*, edited by James Clifford and George E. Marcus, 98–121. Berkeley: University of California Press, 1986.

Cohen, Tom. "Political Thrillers: Hitchcock, de Man, and Secret Agency in the 'Aesthetic State.'" In *Material Events: Paul de Man and the Afterlife of Theory*, edited by Tom Cohen, Barbara Cohen, J. Hillis Miller, and Andrzej Warminski, 114–52. Minneapolis: University of Minnesota Press, 2001.

Cortés, Hernán. *Cartas de relación.* Mexico: Porrúa, 1975.

Coward, Rosalind, and John Ellis. *Language and Materialism: Developments in Semiology and the Theory of the Subject.* London: Routledge and Kegan Paul, 1977.

Culler, Jonathan. *The Pursuit of Signs: Semiotics, Literature, Deconstruction.* Ithaca, N.Y.: Cornell University Press, 1981.

Cvetkovich, Ann. *An Archive of Feelings: Trauma, Sexuality, and Lesbian Public Cultures.* Durham, N.C.: Duke University Press, 2003.

Daston, Lorraine, and Katharine Park. "The Hermaphrodite and the Orders of Nature: Sexual Ambiguity in Early Modern France." In *Premodern Sexualities*, edited by Louise Fradenburg and Carla Freccero, 117–36. New York: Routledge, 1996.

———. *Wonders and the Order of Nature, 1150–1750.* New York: Zone Books, 2001.

D'Avezac, Macaya, ed. *Campagne du navire l'Espoir de Honfleur, 1503–1505: Relation authentique du voyage du Capitaine de Gonneville ès nouvelles terres des Indes.* Paris: Challamel, 1869.

Davidson, Arnold I. "Sex and the Emergence of Sexuality." *Critical Inquiry* 14.1 (1987): 16–48.

Davis, Natalie Zemon. *The Return of Martin Guerre.* Cambridge, Mass.: Harvard University Press, 1983.

———. *Fiction in the Archives: Pardon Tales and their Tellers in Sixteenth-Century France.* Stanford, Calif.: Stanford University Press, 1987.

Debo, Angie. *A History of the Indians of the United States.* 1970. Reprint, Norman: University of Oklahoma Press, 1988.

De Lauretis, Teresa. *Alice Doesn't: Feminism, Semiotics, Cinema.* Bloomington: Indiana University Press, 1984.

———. "Sexual Indifference and Lesbian Representation." *Theater Journal* 40.2 (1988): 155–77. Reprinted in *The Lesbian and Gay Studies Reader*, edited by H. Abelove, M. A. Barale, and D. Halperin, 141–58. New York: Routledge, 1993.

———. "The Stubborn Drive." *Critical Inquiry* 24 (1998): 851–77.

———, ed. *Queer Theory*. Special issue. *Differences: A Journal of Feminist Cultural Studies* 3.2 (1991).

Deleuze, Gilles, and Félix Guattari. *Mille plateaux*. Paris: Minuit, 1980.

———. *A Thousand Plateaus: Capitalism and Schizophrenia*. Translated by Brian Massumi. 1987. Reprint, Minneapolis: University of Minnesota Press, 2000.

Derrida, Jacques. *La voix et le phénomène*. Paris: Presses Universitaires de France, 1967.

———. *De la grammatologie*. Paris: Minuit, 1967.

———. "Structure, Sign, and Play in the Discourse of the Human Sciences." In *The Languages of Criticism and the Sciences of Man: The Structuralist Controversy*, 247–65. Baltimore: Johns Hopkins University Press, 1969.

———. *Positions*. Paris: Minuit, 1972.

———. *Marges de la philosophie*. Paris: Minuit, 1972.

———. *Speech and Phenomena and Other Essays on Husserl's Theory of Signs*. Translated by David B. Allison. Evanston, Ill.: Northwestern University Press, 1973.

———. *Of Grammatology*. Translated by Gayatri Chakravorty Spivak. Baltimore: Johns Hopkins University Press, 1976.

———. "Fors." Preface to *Cryptonymie: Le verbier de l'homme aux loups*, by Nicolas Abraham and Maria Torok. Paris: Aubier Flammarion, 1976.

———. *Eperons: Les styles de Nietzsche/Spurs: Nietzsche's Styles*. Translated by Barbara Harlow. Chicago: University of Chicago Press, 1979.

———. *Positions*. Translated by Alan Bass. Chicago: University of Chicago Press, 1981.

———. *Margins of Philosophy*. Translated by Alan Bass. Chicago: University of Chicago Press, 1982.

———. *Spectres de Marx: L'état de la dette, le travail du deuil et la nouvelle Internationale*. Paris: Editions Galilée, 1993.

———. *Specters of Marx: The State of the Debt, the Work of Mourning, and the New International*. Translated by Peggy Kamuf. New York: Routledge, 1994.

———. "Archive Fever: A Freudian Impression." *Diacritics* 25.2 (1995): 9–63.

———. *Mal d'archive: Une impression freudienne*. Paris: Galilée, 1995.

————. *Archive Fever: A Freudian Impression.* Translated by Eric Preno-
witz. Chicago: University of Chicago Press, 1996.

————. "Marx and Sons." In *Ghostly Demarcations: A Symposium on Jacques
Derrida's* Specters of Marx, edited by Michael Sprinker, 213–69. London: Verso, 1998.

————. "Peines de mort." Interview with Elisabeth Roudinesco. In *De
Quoi demain . . . dialogue,* 256–58. Paris: Fayard/Galilée, 2001.

Derrida, Jacques, and Elisabeth Roudinesco. *For What Tomorrow—: A Dialogue.* Translated by Jeff Fort. Stanford, Calif.: Stanford University
Press, 2004.

Destins du cannibalisme. Edited by J.-B. Pontalis. Special issue. *Nouvelle revue de psychanalyse* 6 (1972).

Diamond, Stanley. *In Search of the Primitive: A Critique of Civilization.* New
Brunswick, N.J.: E. P. Dutton, 1974.

Díaz, Bernal. *The Conquest of New Spain.* Translated by J. M. Cohen.
Middlesex, England: Penguin Classics, 1963.

————. *Historia verdadera de la conquista de México.* Madrid: Espasa-Calpe,
1975.

Dinshaw, Carolyn. "A Kiss Is Just a Kiss: Heterosexuality and Its Con-
solations in *Sir Gawain and the Green Knight.*" *Diacritics* 24.2–3 (1994):
205–26.

————. "Chaucer's Queer Touches/A Queer Touches Chaucer." *Exem-
plaria* 7.1 (1995): 75–92.

————. *Getting Medieval: Sexualities and Communities, Pre- and Postmodern.*
Durham, N.C.: Duke University Press, 1999.

Dollimore, Jonathan. *Sexual Dissidence: Augustine to Wilde, Freud to Foucault.* Oxford: Clarendon, 1991.

Donahue, Charles, Jr. "The Canon Law on the Formation of Marriage
and Social Practice in the Later Middle Ages." *Journal of Family History*
8.2 (1983): 144–56.

Duggan, Lisa. "Queering the State." *Social Text* 39 (1994): 1–14.

————. "The Discipline Problem: Queer Theory Meets Lesbian and Gay
History." *GLQ: A Journal of Lesbian and Gay Studies* 2 (1995): 179–91.

————. "The Theory Wars, or, Who's Afraid of Judith Butler?" *Journal
of Women's History* 10 (1998): 9–19.

Dupront, Alphonse. "Langage et histoire." XIIIe Congrès international
des sciences historiques. Moscow: Editions de l'Université de Varso-
vie, 1975.

Durling, Robert. *Petrarch's Lyric Poems: The "Rime Sparse" and Other Lyrics.*
Cambridge, Mass.: Harvard University Press, 1976.

Duval, Edwin. "Lessons of the New World: Design and Meaning in Montaigne's 'Des cannibales' (I:31) and 'Des coches' (III:6)." *Yale French Studies* 64 (1983): 95–112.

———. *The Design of Rabelais's* Pantagruel. New Haven, Conn.: Yale University Press, 1991.

Ebert, Teresa. "The Matter of Materialism." In *The Material Queer: A LesBiGay Cultural Studies Reader*, edited by Donald Morton, 352–61. Boulder, Colo.: Westview Press, 1996.

Edleman, Lee. "Queer Theory: Unstating Desire." *GLQ: A Journal of Lesbian and Gay Studies* 2.4 (1995): 343–48.

Engels, Friedrich. *The Origin of the Family, Private Property and the State.* New York: Viking Penguin, 1986.

Enterline, Lynn. *The Rhetoric of the Body from Ovid to Shakespeare.* Cambridge: Cambridge University Press, 2000.

Epstein, Barbara. "Why Poststructuralism Is a Dead End for Progressive Thought." *Socialist Review* 25.2 (1995): 83–119.

Eribon, Didier. *Michel Foucault (1926–1984).* Paris: Flammarion, 1989.

———. *Les études gay et lesbiennes: Textes réunis par Didier Eribon.* Paris: Centre G. Pompidou, 1998.

———. "Michel Foucault's Histories of Sexuality." Translated by Michael Lucey. *GLQ: A Journal of Lesbian and Gay Studies* 7 (2001): 31–86.

Etheridge, Melissa. *Melissa Etheridge.* Produced by Craig Krampf, Kevin McCormick, Melissa Etheridge, and Niko Bolas. Words and music by Melissa Etheridge. Island Records, Inc., 1988.

———. *Brave and Crazy.* Produced by Kevin McCormick, Niko Bolas, Melissa Etheridge. Words and music by Melissa Etheridge. Island Records, Inc., 1989.

———. *Never Enough.* Produced by Kevin McCormick and Melissa Etheridge. Words and music by Melissa Etheridge. Island Records, Inc., 1992.

———. *Yes I Am.* Produced by Hugh Padgham and Melissa Etheridge. Words and music by Melissa Etheridge. Island Records, Inc., 1993.

———. *Your Little Secret.* Produced by Hugh Padgham and Melissa Etheridge. Words and music by Melissa Etheridge. Island Records, Inc., 1995.

Fabian, Johannes. *Time and the Other: How Anthropology Makes Its Object.* New York: Columbia University Press, 1983.

Ferguson, Margaret. "Recreating the Rules of the Game: Marguerite de Navarre's *Heptaméron.*" In *Creative Imitation: New Essays on Renaissance Literature in Honor of Thomas M. Greene*, edited by David Quint, Margaret W. Ferguson, G. W. Pigman III, and Wayne A. Rebhorn, 153–87. Binghamton: State University of New York at Binghamton, Center for Medieval and Renaissance Studies, 1992.

Foucault, Michel. *Madness and Civilization: A History of Insanity in the Age of Reason*. Translated by Richard Howard. 1965. Reprint, New York: Pantheon Books, 1988.

———. *Les mots et les choses: Une archéologie des sciences humaines*. Paris: Gallimard, 1966.

———. *The Order of Things: An Archeology of the Human Sciences*. New York: Random House, 1970.

———. *Surveiller et punir: Naissance de la prison*. Paris: Gallimard, 1975.

———. *Histoire de la folie à l'âge classique*. Paris: Gallimard, 1976.

———. *Histoire de la sexualité I: La volonté de savoir*. Paris: Gallimard, 1976.

———. *Discipline and Punish: The Birth of the Prison*. Translated by Alan Sheridan. New York: Vintage Books, 1979.

———. *The History of Sexuality, Volume I: An Introduction*. Translated by Robert Hurley. New York: Vintage, 1980.

Fradenburg, Louise, and Carla Freccero. "Caxton, Foucault, and the Pleasures of History." In *Premodern Sexualities*, edited by Louise Fradenburg and Carla Freccero, xiii–xxiv. New York: Routledge, 1996.

Fradenburg, L. O. Aranye. *Sacrifice Your Love: Psychoanalysis, Historicism, Chaucer*. Minneapolis: University of Minnesota Press, 2002.

Fraser, Nancy. "Heterosexism, Misrecognition, and Capitalism." *Social Text* 52/53 (1997): 279–89.

Freccero, Carla. "Margaret of Navarre." In *A New History of French Literature*, edited by Denis Hollier, 145–48. Cambridge, Mass.: Harvard University Press, 1989.

———. "Notes of a Post–Sex Wars Theorizer." In *Conflicts in Feminism*, edited by Marianne Hirsch and Evelyn Fox Keller, 305–25. New York: Routledge, 1990.

———. *Father Figures: Genealogy and Narrative Structure in Rabelais*. Ithaca, N.Y.: Cornell University Press, 1991.

———. "Rape's Disfiguring Figures: Marguerite de Navarre's *Heptameron*, Day 1:10." In *Rape and Representation*, edited by Lynn A. Higgins and Brenda R. Silver, 227–47. New York: Columbia University Press, 1991.

———. "Marguerite de Navarre and the Politics of Maternal Sovereignty." *Cosmos* 7 (1992): 132–49.

———. "Cannibalism, Homophobia, Women: Montaigne's 'Des Cannibales' and 'De L'Amitié.'" In *Women, "Race," and Writing in the Early*

Modern Period, edited by Margo Hendricks and Patricia Parker, 73–83. New York: Routledge, 1994.

———. "Practicing Queer Philology with Marguerite de Navarre: Nationalism and the Castigation of Desire." In *Queering the Renaissance*, edited by Jonathan Goldberg, 107–23. Durham, N.C.: Duke University Press, 1994.

———. "Historical Violence, Censorship, and the Serial Killer: The Case of *American Psycho*." In *Censorship*, edited by George Van den Abbeele. Special issue, *Diacritics* 27.2 (1997): 44–58.

———. *Popular Culture: An Introduction*. New York: New York University Press, 1998.

———. "Acts, Identities, and Sexuality's (Pre)Modern Regimes." *Journal of Women's History* 11.2 (1999): 186–92.

———. "Early Modern Psychoanalytics: Montaigne and the Melancholic Subject of Humanism." *Qui parle* 11.2 (1999): 89–114.

———. "Louise Labé's Feminist Poetics." In *Distant Voices Still Heard: Contemporary Readings of French Renaissance Literature*, edited by John O'Brien and Malcolm Quainton, 107–22. Liverpool: Liverpool University Press, 2000.

———. "Archives in the Fiction: Marguerite de Navarre's *Heptaméron*." In *Rhetoric and Law in Early Modern Europe*, edited by Victoria Kahn and Lorna Hutson, 73–94. New Haven, Conn.: Yale University Press, 2001.

———. "Ovidian Subjectivities in Early Modern Lyric: Identification and Desire in Petrarch and Louise Labé." In *Ovid and the Renaissance Body*, edited by Goran Stanivukovic, 21–37. New York: Routledge, 2001.

———. "Toward a Psychoanalytics of Historiography: Michel de Certeau's Early Modern Encounters." In *Michel de Certeau—In the Plural*, edited by Ian Buchanan. Special issue, *South Atlantic Quarterly* 100 (2001): 365–79.

———. "Heteroerotic Homoeroticism: Jean de Léry and the 'New World Man.'" In *The Rhetoric of the Other: Lesbian and Gay Strategies of Resistance in French and Francophone Contexts*, edited by Martine Antle and Dominique Fisher, 101–14. New Orleans: University Press of the South, 2002.

———. "'They Are All Sodomites!'" *Signs: Journal of Women in Culture and Society* 28 (2002): 453–55.

Freccero, John. "The Fig Tree and the Laurel: Petrarch's Poetics." *Diacritics* 5 (1975): 34–40.

Freud, Sigmund. "Some Psychological Consequences of the Anatomical Distinction between the Sexes" (1925). In *Standard Edition of the Complete Psychological Works of Sigmund Freud*, edited by James Strachey, 19:243–58. London: Hogarth, 1961.

————. "From the History of An Infantile Neurosis" (1918). In *Standard Edition of the Complete Psychological Works of Sigmund Freud*, edited by James Strachey, 17:48–121. London: Hogarth, 1961.

Fuss, Diana, ed. *Inside/Out: Lesbian Theories, Gay Theories*. New York: Routledge, 1991.

Gaignebet, Claude. *Le Coeur mangé. Récits érotiques et courtois des XIIe et XIIIe siècles*. Paris: Stock, 1979.

Gallagher, Catherine, and Stephen Greenblatt. *Practicing New Historicism*. Chicago: University of Chicago Press, 2000.

Gates, Henry Louis, Jr. "'What's Love Got to Do with It?' Critical Theory, Integrity, and the Black Idiom." *New Literary History* 18 (1987): 345–62.

Gaunt, Simon. "Straight Minds/'Queer' Wishes in Old French Hagiography: *La vie de Sainte Euphrosine*." In *Premodern Sexualities*, edited by Louise Fradenburg and Carla Freccero, 155–73. New York: Routledge, 1996.

Gaylard, Susan. "The Crisis of Word and Deed in *Decameron* V 10." In *The Italian Novella*, edited by Gloria Allaire, 33–48. New York: Routledge, 2003.

Goldberg, Jonathan. *Sodometries: Renaissance Texts, Modern Sexualities*. Stanford, Calif.: Stanford University Press, 1992.

————. "The History That Will Be." In *Premodern Sexualities*, edited by Louise Fradenburg and Carla Freccero, 3–21. New York: Routledge, 1996.

————. "The Anus in *Coriolanus*." In *Historicism, Psychoanalysis, and Early Modern Culture*, edited by Carla Mazzio and Douglas Trevor, 260–71. New York: Routledge, 2000.

————, ed. *Queering the Renaissance*. Durham, N.C.: Duke University Press, 1994.

Gordon, Avery. *Ghostly Matters: Haunting and the Sociological Imagination*. Minneapolis: University of Minnesota Press, 1997.

Gottlieb, Beatrice. "The Meaning of Clandestine Marriage." In *Family and Sexuality in French History*, edited by Robert Wheaton and Tamara K. Hareven, 49–83. Philadelphia: University of Pennsylvania Press, 1980.

Gratian. *Decretum Gratiani*. Edited by J. P. Migne. Paris: Garnier, 1912.

Greenblatt, Stephen. "Invisible Bullets: Renaissance Authority and Its Subversion, *Henry IV* and *Henry V.*" In *Political Shakespeare*, edited by Jonathan Dollimore and Alan Sinfield, 18–47. Ithaca, N.Y.: Cornell University Press, 1985.

———. *Marvelous Possessions: The Wonder of the New World.* Chicago: University of Chicago Press, 1991.

———. "Psychoanalysis and Renaissance Culture." In *Literary Theory/Renaissance Texts*, edited by Patricia Parker and David Quint. Baltimore: Johns Hopkins University Press, 1986.

Greene, Jody. "New Historicism and Its New World Discoveries." *Yale Journal of Criticism* 4 (1991): 163–98.

Greene, Roland. *Unrequited Conquests: Love and Empire in the Colonial Americas.* Chicago: University of Chicago Press, 1999.

Grewal, Inderpal. " 'Women's Rights as Human Rights': Feminist Practices, Global Feminism, and Human Rights Regimes in Transnationality." *Citizenship Studies* 3 (1999): 337–54.

Grosz, Elizabeth. "Bodies and Pleasures in Queer Theory." In *Who Can Speak? Authority and Critical Identity*, edited by Judith Roof and Robyn Wiegman, 221–30. Urbana: University of Illinois Press, 1995.

———. "Ontology and Equivocation: Derrida's Politics of Sexual Difference." In *Feminist Interpretations of Jacques Derrida*, edited by Nancy J. Holland, 73–101. University Park: Pennsylvania State University Press, 1997.

Gubar, Susan. " 'The Blank Page' and the Issues of Female Creativity." *Critical Inquiry* 8 (1981): 243–63.

———. "What Ails Feminist Criticism?" *Critical Inquiry* 24.4 (1998): 878–902.

Guillory, John. *Cultural Capital: The Problem of Literary Canon Formation.* Chicago: University of Chicago Press, 1993.

Halberstam, Judith. "Imagined Violence/Queer Violence: Representation, Rage, and Resistance." *Social Text* 37 (1993): 187–201.

———. "F2M: The Making of Female Masculinity." In *The Lesbian Postmodern*, edited by Laura Doan, 210–28. New York: Columbia University Press, 1994.

———. "Lesbian Masculinity; or, Even Stone Butches Get the Blues." *Women and Performance: A Journal of Feminist Theory* 8.2 (1996): 61–73.

———. "Transgender Butch: Butch/FTM Border Wars and the Masculine Continuum." In *The Transgender Issue*, edited by Susan Stryker. Special issue, *GLQ: A Journal of Lesbian and Gay Studies* 4 (1998): 287–310.

———. *Female Masculinity*. Durham, N.C.: Duke University Press, 1998.

———. "Telling Tales: Brandon Teena, Billy Tipton, and Transgender Biography." *A/B: Auto/Biography Studies* 15 (2000): 62–81.

Hale, C. Jacob. "Consuming the Living, Dis(re)membering the Dead in the Butch/FTM Borderlands." In *The Transgender Issue*, edited by Susan Stryker. Special issue, *GLQ: A Journal of Lesbian and Gay Studies* 4 (1998): 311–49.

Halperin, David. *One Hundred Years of Homosexuality and Other Essays on Greek Love*. New York: Routledge, 1990.

———. "Forgetting Foucault: Acts, Identities and the History of Sexuality." *Representations* 63 (1998): 93–120.

———. "How to Do the History of Male Homosexuality." *GLQ: A Journal of Lesbian and Gay Studies* 6 (2000): 87–123.

———. *How to Do the History of Homosexuality*. Chicago: University of Chicago Press, 2002.

Hampton, Timothy. *Literature and Nation in the Sixteenth Century: Inventing Renaissance France*. Ithaca, N.Y.: Cornell University Press, 2001.

Hanley, Sarah. "Family and State in Early Modern France: The Marriage Pact." In *Connecting Spheres: Women in the Western World, 1500 to the Present*, edited by Marilyn Boxer and Jean Quataert, 53–63. New York: Oxford University Press, 1987.

———. "The Monarchic State in Early Modern France: Marital Regime Government and Male Right." In *Politics, Ideology, and the Law in Early Modern Europe: Essays in Honor of J. H. M. Salmon*, edited by Adrianna Bakos, 107–26. Rochester, N.Y.: University of Rochester Press, 1994.

———. "La loi salique." In *Encyclopédie politique et historique des femmes: Europe, Amérique du Nord*, 11–30. Paris: Presses Universitaires de France, 1996.

Haraway, Donna. *Simians, Cyborgs, and Women: The Reinvention of Nature*. New York: Routledge, 1991.

———. "The Promises of Monsters: A Regenerative Politics for Inappropriate/d Others." In *Cultural Studies*, edited by Lawrence Grossberg, Cary Nelson, Paula A. Treichler, with Linda Baughman and John Macgregor Wise, 295–337. New York: Routledge, 1992.

Hartley, L. P. *The Go-Between*. London: H. Hamilton, 1953.

Hocquenghem, Guy. *Le désir homosexuel*. Paris: Editions Universitaires, 1972.

———. *Homosexual Desire*. Translated by Daniella Dangoor. London: Allison and Busby, 1978.

hooks, bell. *Feminist Theory: From Margin to Center*. Boston: South End, 1984.

Hope, Trevor. "Melancholic Modernity: The Hom(m)osexual Symptom and the Homosocial Corpse." *Differences: A Journal of Feminist Cultural Studies* 6.2–3 (1994): 174–98.

———. "Sexual Indifference and the Homosexual Male Imaginary." *Diacritics: A Review of Contemporary Criticism* 24.2–3 (1994): 169–83.

Hulme, Peter. *Colonial Encounters: Europe and the Native Caribbean, 1492–1797*. 1986. Reprint, London: Methuen, 1992.

Irigaray, Luce. *Ce sexe qui n'en est pas un*. Paris: Minuit, 1977.

———. *This Sex Which Is Not One*. Translated by Catherine Porter with Carolyn Burke. Ithaca, N.Y.: Cornell University Press, 1985.

Jackson, Earl, Jr. *Strategies of Deviance: Studies in Gay Male Representation*. Bloomington: Indiana University Press, 1995.

Jackson, Richard A. "Peers of France and Princes of the Blood." *French Historical Studies* 7.1 (1971): 27–46.

Jagose, Annamarie. *Queer Theory: An Introduction*. New York: New York University Press, 1996.

Jameson, Fredric. *The Political Unconscious: Narrative as a Socially Symbolic Act*. Ithaca, N.Y.: Cornell University Press, 1981.

———. "Marx's Purloined Letter." In *Ghostly Demarcations: A Symposium on Jacques Derrida's* Specters of Marx, edited by Michael Sprinker, 26–67. London: Verso, 1998.

Jardine, Alice. *Gynesis: Configurations of Women and Modernity*. Ithaca, N.Y.: Cornell University Press, 1985.

Jardine, Lisa. *Still Harping on Daughters: Women and Drama in the Age of Shakespeare*. Sussex: Harvester Press; Totowa, N.J.: Barnes & Noble, 1983.

———. *Worldly Goods*. London: Macmillan, 1996.

Jayawardena, Kumari. *Feminism and Nationalism in the Third World*. London: Zed, 1986.

Jed, Stephanie. *Chaste Thinking: The Rape of Lucretia and the Birth of Humanism*. Bloomington: Indiana University Press, 1989.

Johnson, Barbara. *The Critical Difference: Essays in the Contemporary Rhetoric of Reading*. Baltimore: Johns Hopkins University Press, 1980.

———. *A World of Difference*. Baltimore: Johns Hopkins University Press, 1987.

Jones, Ann Rosalind. "City Women and Their Audiences: Louise Labé and Veronica Franco." In *Rewriting the Renaissance: The Discourse of Sexual Difference in Early Modern Europe*, edited by Margaret W. Ferguson, Maureen Quilligan, and Nancy J. Vickers, 299–316. Chicago: University of Chicago Press, 1986.

———. *The Currency of Eros: Women's Love Lyric in Europe, 1540–1620*. Bloomington: Indiana University Press, 1990.

———. " 'Blond chef, grande conqueste': Feminist Theories of the Gaze, the Blazon Anatomique and Louise Labé's Sonnet 6." In *Distant Voices Still Heard: Contemporary Readings of French Renaissance Literature*, edited by John O'Brien and Malcolm Quainton, 85–106. Liverpool: Liverpool University Press, 2000.

Joplin, Patricia Klindienst. "The Voice of the Shuttle Is Ours." In *Rape and Representation*, edited by Lynn Higgins and Brenda Silver, 35–64. New York: Columbia University Press, 1991.

Joyce, Joyce A. "The Black Canon: Reconstructing Black American Literary Criticism." *New Literary History* 18 (1987): 335–44.

———. " 'Who the Cap Fit': Unconsciousness and Unconscionableness in the Criticism of Houston A. Baker, Jr., and Henry Louis Gates, Jr." *New Literary History* 18 (1987): 371–84.

Kamuf, Peggy. "Replacing Feminist Criticism." In *Conflicts in Feminism*, edited by Marianne Hirsch and Evelyn Fox Keller, 105–11. New York: Routledge, 1990.

———. "Deconstruction and Feminism: A Repetition." In *Feminist Interpretations of Jacques Derrida*, edited by Nancy J. Holland, 103–26. University Park: Pennsylvania University Press, 1997.

———. *The Division of Literature: The University in Deconstruction*. Chicago: University of Chicago Press, 1997.

———, ed. *A Derrida Reader: Between the Blinds*. New York: Columbia University Press, 1991.

Kamuf, Peggy, and Nancy K. Miller. "Parisian Letters: Between Feminism and Deconstruction." In *Conflicts in Feminism*, edited by Marianne Hirsch and Evelyn Fox Keller, 121–33. New York: Routledge, 1990.

Kaplan, Cora. *Sea Changes: Culture and Feminism*. London: Verso, 1986.

Karras, Ruth Mazo. "Prostitution and the Question of Sexual Identity in Medieval Europe." *Journal of Women's History* 11 (1999): 159–77.

———. "Response: Identity, Sexuality, and History." *Journal of Women's History* 11 (1999): 193–98.

Kelly, Joan. "Did Women Have a Renaissance?" In *Women, History, and Theory*, 19–50. Chicago: University of Chicago Press, 1984.

Kilgour, Maggie. *From Communion to Cannibalism: An Anatomy of Metaphors of Incorporation*. Princeton, N.J.: Princeton University Press, 1990.

Kinoshita, Sharon. "'Pagans Are Wrong and Christians Are Right': Alterity, Gender and Nation in the *Chanson de Roland.*" *Journal of Medieval and Early Modern Studies* 31 (2001): 79–111.

Klapisch-Zuber, Christiane. *Women, Family, and Ritual in Renaissance Italy.* Translated by Lydia G. Cochrane. Chicago: University of Chicago Press, 1985.

Labé, Louise. *Oeuvres complètes.* Edited by François Rigolot. Paris: Flammarion, 1986.

La Boétie, Etienne de. *Discours de la servitude volontaire.* Edited by Simone Goyard-Fabre. Paris: Garnier Flammarion, 1983.

Lane, Christopher. "The Poverty of Context: Historicism and Nonmimetic Fiction." *PMLA* 118 (2003): 450–69.

Laplanche, Jean, and J.-B. Pontalis. *Vocabulaire de la psychanalyse.* Paris: Presses Universitaires de France, 1967.

———. *The Language of Psychoanalysis.* Translated by Donald Nicholson-Smith. New York: Norton, 1973.

Las Casas, Bartolomé de. *The Devastation of the Indies: A Brief Account.* Translated by Herma Briffaut, introduced by Bill M. Donovan. 1974. Reprint, Baltimore: Johns Hopkins University Press, 1992.

———. *Brevísima relación de la destruición de las Indias.* Edited by André Saint-Lu. Madrid: Ediciones Cátedra, 1999.

Latour, Bruno. *Nous n'avons jamais été modernes: Essai d'anthropologie symétrique.* Paris: La Découverte, 1991.

———. *We Have Never Been Modern.* Translated by Catherine Porter. Cambridge, Mass.: Harvard University Press, 1993.

Left Conservatism: A Workshop. Boundary 2 26.3 (1999): 1–61.

Léry, Jean de. *Histoire d'un voyage en terre de Brésil.* 1578. Edited by Jean-Claude Morisot. Geneva: Droz, 1975.

———. *Histoire d'un voyage en terre de Brésil.* 1578. Edited by Frank Lestringant. Paris: Le Livre de Poche, 1994.

———. *History of a Voyage to the Land of Brazil.* Edited and translated by Janet Whatley. Berkeley: University of California Press, 1990.

Lestringant, Frank. *Le cannibale: Grandeur et decadence.* Paris: Perrin, 1994.

———. *Cannibals: The Discovery and Representation of the Cannibal from Columbus to Jules Verne.* Translated by Rosemary Morris. Berkeley: University of California Press, 1997.

Lévi-Strauss, Claude. *Tristes tropiques.* Paris: Plon, 1955.

———. *Les structures élémentaires de la parenté.* Paris: La Haye, Mouton, 1967.

———. *The Elementary Structures of Kinship.* Edited and translated by

James Harle Bell, John Richard von Sturmer, and Rodney Needham. Boston: Beacon, 1969.

Lochrie, Karma. "Don't Ask, Don't Tell: Murderous Plots and Medieval Secrets." In *Premodern Sexualities*, edited by Louise Fradenburg and Carla Freccero, 137–52. New York: Routledge, 1996.

———. *Covert Operations: The Medieval Uses of Secrecy*. Philadelphia: University of Pennsylvania Press, 1999.

Lucey, Michael. "Kinship, Economics, and Queer Sexuality in Balzac's *Old Goriot.*" In *Approaches to Teaching Balzac's* Old Goriot, edited by Michal Peled Ginsburg, 126–33. New York: Modern Language Association of America, 2000.

———. *The Misfit of the Family: Balzac and the Social Forms of Sexuality*. Durham, N.C.: Duke University Press, 2003.

———, trans. "Michel Foucault's Histories of Sexuality." *GLQ: A Journal of Lesbian and Gay Studies* 7.1 (2001): 31–72.

Lupton, Julia Reinhard. "Secularization and Its Symptoms: Boccaccio's *Decameron.*" In *Repossessions: Psychoanalysis and the Phantasms of Early Modern Culture*, edited by Timothy Murray and Alan K. Smith, 3–22. Minneapolis: University of Minnesota Press, 1998.

Lyons, John. *Exemplum: The Rhetoric of Example in Early Modern France and Italy*. Princeton, N.J.: Princeton University Press, 1989.

MacCannell, Juliet Flower. *The Regime of the Brother: After the Patriarchy*. London: Routledge, 1991.

Marcus, Leah. *Puzzling Shakespeare*. Berkeley: University of California Press, 1988.

———. "Renaissance/Early Modern Studies." In *Redrawing the Boundaries: The Transformation of English and American Literary Studies*, edited by Stephen Greenblatt and Giles Gunn, 41–63. New York: Modern Language Association, 1992.

Martin, Biddy. "Extraordinary Homosexuals and the Fear of Being Ordinary." *Differences: A Journal of Feminist Cultural Studies* 6.2–3 (1994): 100–125.

Mazzio, Carla, and Douglas Trevor, eds. *Historicism, Psychoanalysis, and Early Modern Culture*. New York: Routledge, 2000.

McClintock, Anne. *Imperial Leather: Race, Gender and Sexuality in the Colonial Contest*. New York: Routledge, 1995.

Menocal, Maria Rosa. *Shards of Love: Exile and the Origins of the Lyric*. Durham, N.C.: Duke University Press, 1994.

Mies, Maria. *Patriarchy and Accumulation on a World Scale: Women in the International Division of Labour*. London: Zed Books, 1986.

Mignolo, Walter. *The Darker Side of the Renaissance: Literacy, Territory, and Colonization.* 1999. Reprint, Ann Arbor: University of Michigan Press, 2001.

Minh-ha, Trinh T. *Woman, Native, Other: Writing Postcoloniality and Feminism.* Bloomington: Indiana University Press, 1989.

Montaigne, Michel de. *Oeuvres complètes.* Edited by Maurice Rat. Paris: Gallimard, 1962.

Mooney, James. *The Ghost-Dance Religion and the Sioux Outbreak of 1890.* Glorieta, N. Mex.: Rio Grande, 1973.

Morton, Donald. "Birth of the Cyberqueer." *PMLA* 110 (1995): 369–81.

——. "Changing the Terms: (Virtual) Desire and (Actual) Reality." In *The Material Queer: A LesBiGay Cultural Studies Reader*, edited by Donald Morton, 1–33. Boulder, Colo.: Westview, 1996.

——, ed. *The Material Queer: A LesBiGay Cultural Studies Reader.* Boulder, Colo.: Westview, 1996.

Mosse, George L. *Nationalism and Sexuality: Middle-Class Morality and Sexual Norms in Modern Europe.* Madison: University of Wisconsin Press, 1988.

Muñoz, José Esteban. *Disidentifications: Queers of Color and the Performance of Politics.* Minneapolis: University of Minnesota Press, 1999.

Murray, Timothy, and Alan K. Smith, eds. *Repossessions: Psychoanalysis and the Phantasms of Early Modern Culture.* Minneapolis: University of Minnesota Press, 1998.

Nakam, Géralde, ed. *Au lendemain de la Saint-Barthélemy, guerre civile et famine*: Histoire mémorable du siège de Sancerre *de Jean de Léry.* Paris: Editions Anthropos, 1975.

Navarre, Marguerite de. *L'heptaméron.* Edited by Michel François. Paris: Garnier, 1967.

——. *The Heptameron.* Edited and translated by P. A. Chilton. Middlesex, England: Penguin, 1984.

Neuber, Jen. "Jean de Léry's Queer Identifications: Savage Warfare and Technologies of Desire in *History of a Voyage to the Land of Brazil.*" Unpublished paper.

Nickson, Chris. *Melissa Etheridge: The Only One.* New York: St. Martin's Griffin, 1997.

Noonan, John T., Jr. "Marriage in the Middle Ages: 1, Power to Choose." *Viator: Medieval and Renaissance Studies* 4 (1973): 419–34.

Osborne, Peter. *The Politics of Time: Modernity and Avant-garde.* London: Verso, 1995.

Ovid [Publius Ovidius Naso]. *Metamorphoses*, vol. 1. Cambridge, Mass.: Harvard University Press, 1971.

Pagden, Anthony. *European Encounters with the New World: From Renaissance to Romanticism*. New Haven, Conn.: Yale University Press, 1993.

Parker, Andrew, Mary Russo, Doris Sommer, and Patricia Yaeger, eds. *Nationalisms and Sexualities*. New York: Routledge, 1992.

Pastor, Beatriz. "Silence and Writing: The History of the Conquest." In *1492–1992: Re/Discovering Colonial Writing, Hispanic Issues 4*, edited by René Jara and Nicholas Spadaccini, 121–63. 1989. Reprint, Minneapolis: University of Minnesota Press, 1991.

Patel, Geeta, and Kevin Kopelson. *Inqueery/Intheory/Indeed*. Special issue. *GLQ: A Journal of Lesbian and Gay Studies* 2 (1995).

Patterson, Lee. "The Place of the Modern in the Late Middle Ages." In *The Challenge of Periodization: Old Paradigms and New Perspectives*, edited by Lawrence Besserman, 51–66. New York: Garland, 1996.

Patton, Cindy. "Tremble, Hetero Swine!" In *Fear of a Queer Planet: Queer Politics and Social Theory*, edited by Michael Warner, 143–77. Minneapolis: University of Minnesota Press, 1993.

Pearson, Joseph, ed. *Fearless Speech*. Los Angeles: Semiotext(e), 2001.

Pollitt, Katha. "Pomolotov Cocktail." *Nation*, June 10, 1996, 9.

Poovey, Mary. *Uneven Developments: The Ideological Work of Gender in Mid-Victorian England*. Chicago: University of Chicago Press, 1988.

Pratt, Mary Louise. "Americanizing Cultural Theory." Conference at the Center for Cultural Studies, University of California, Santa Cruz, April 3, 1992.

Prosser, Jay. *Second Skins: The Body Narratives of Transsexuality*. New York: Columbia University Press, 1998.

Quilligan, Maureen. "Incest and Agency: The Case of Elizabeth I." In *Generation and Degeneration: Tropes of Reproduction in Literature and History from Antiquity to Early Modern Europe*, edited by Valeria Finucci and Kevin Brownlee, 209–31. Durham, N.C.: Duke University Press, 2001.

Quint, David. "A Reconsideration of Montaigne's 'Des Cannibales.'" *Modern Language Quarterly* 51 (1990): 459–89.

Rafael, Vicente L. *White Love and Other Events in Filippino History*. Durham, N.C.: Duke University Press, 2000.

Raffles, Hugh. *In Amazonia: A Natural History*. Princeton, N.J.: Princeton University Press, 2002.

Renan, Ernest. "Qu'est-ce qu'une nation?" In *Oeuvres complètes*, 1:887–906. Paris: Calmann-Lévy, 1947–61.

Richards, Jeffrey. *Sex, Dissidence, and Damnation: Minority Groups in the Middle Ages*. London: Routledge, 1990.

Rigolot, François. "Quel 'genre' d'amour pour Louise Labé?" *Poétique* 55 (1983): 303–17.

———. "Gender vs. Sex Difference in Louise Labe's Grammar of Love." In *Rewriting the Renaissance: The Discourses of Sexual Difference in Early Modern Europe*, edited by Margaret W. Ferguson, Maureen Quilligan, and Nancy J. Vickers, 287–98. Chicago: University of Chicago Press, 1986.

Riley, Denise. *"Am I That Name?" Feminism and the Category of "Women" in History*. Minneapolis: University of Minnesota Press, 1988.

Roach, Joseph. *Cities of the Dead: Circum-Atlantic Performance*. New York: Columbia University Press, 1996.

Rocke, Michael. *Forbidden Friendships: Homosexuality and Male Culture in Renaissance Florence*. New York: Oxford University Press, 1996.

Rofel, Lisa. "Qualities of Desire: Imagining Gay Identities in China." *GLQ: A Journal of Gay and Lesbian Studies* 5 (1999): 451–74.

Rosaldo, Michelle. "The Use and Abuse of Anthropology: Reflections on Feminism and Cross-Cultural Understanding." *Signs* 5.3 (1980): 389–417.

Rose, Tricia. *Longing to Tell: Black Women's Stories of Sexuality and Intimacy*. New York: Farrar, Straus, Giroux, 2003.

Rosenberg, Jordana. "Butler's 'Lesbian Phallus'; or, What Can Deconstruction Feel?" *GLQ: A Journal of Lesbian and Gay Studies* 9 (2003): 393–414.

Rubin, Gayle. "The Traffic in Women: Notes on the 'Political Economy' of Sex." In *Toward an Anthropology of Women*, edited by Rayna R. Reiter, 157–210. New York: Monthly Review Press, 1975.

———. "Thinking Sex." In *Pleasure and Danger: Exploring Female Sexuality*, edited by Carole S. Vance, 267–319. Boston: Routledge and Kegan Paul, 1984. Reprinted in *The Lesbian and Gay Studies Reader*, edited by Henry Abelove, Michèle Aina Barale, and David M. Halperin, 3–44. New York: Routledge, 1993.

———. "Sexual Traffic." Interview with Judith Butler. *Differences: A Journal of Feminist Cultural Studies* 6.2–3 (1994): 62–99.

Ruggiero, Guido. *The Boundaries of Eros: Sex Crime and Sexuality in Renaissance Venice*. New York: Oxford University Press, 1985.

Saakana, Amon Saba. "Mythology and History: An Afrocentric Perspective of the World." *Third Text* 3–4 (1988): 143–50.

Schachter, Marc. *"Voluntary Servitude" and the Politics of Friendship: Plato,*

Ariosto, La Boétie, Montaigne. PhD diss., University of California, Santa Cruz, 2000.

Schiesari, Juliana. *The Gendering of Melancholia: Feminism, Psychoanalysis, and the Symbolics of Loss in Renaissance Literature*. Ithaca, N.Y.: Cornell University Press, 1992.

Scott, Joan. "Deconstructing Equality-Versus-Difference; or, the Uses of Poststructuralist Theory for Feminism." In *Conflicts in Feminism*, edited by Marianne Hirsch and Evelyn Fox Keller, 134–48. New York: Routledge, 1990.

———. "Experience." In *Feminists Theorize the Political*, edited by Judith Butler and Joan Scott, 22–40. New York: Routledge, 1992.

Sedgwick, Eve Kosofsky. *Between Men: English Literature and Male Homosocial Desire*. New York: Columbia University Press, 1985.

———. *Epistemology of the Closet*. Berkeley: University of California Press, 1990.

———. "Queer Performativity: Henry James' *The Art of the Novel*." *GLQ: A Journal of Lesbian and Gay Studies* 1 (1993): 1–16.

Silverman, Kaja. *Male Subjectivity at the Margins*. New York: Routledge, 1992.

Sollors, Werner. *Beyond Ethnicity: Consent and Descent in American Culture*. New York: Oxford University Press, 1986.

Spackman, Barbara. " 'Inter musam et ursam moritur': Folengo and the Gaping 'Other' Mouth." In *Refiguring Woman: Perspectives on Gender and the Italian Renaissance*, edited by Marilyn Migiel and Juliana Schiesari, 19–34. Ithaca, N.Y.: Cornell University Press, 1991.

Spillers, Hortense. "Interstices: A Small Drama of Words." In *Pleasure and Danger: Exploring Female Sexuality*, edited by Carole S. Vance, 73–100. Boston: Routledge and Kegan Paul, 1984.

Spivak, Gayatri. "Ghostwriting." *Diacritics* 25.2 (1995): 65–84.

———. "Echo." In *The Spivak Reader: Selected Works of Gayatri Chakravorty Spivak*, edited by Donna Landry and Gerald MacLean, 175–202. New York: Routledge, 1996.

Spivak, Gayatri, with Ellen Rooney. "In A Word" (Interview). *Differences: A Journal of Feminist Cultural Studies* 1.2 (1989): 124–56.

Stocchi, Manlio Pastore. "Un antecedente latino-medievale di Pietro di Vinciolo (*Decameron*, V 10)." *Studi sul Boccaccio* 1 (1963): 349–62.

Stoler, Ann Laura. *Race and the Education of Desire: Foucault's* History of Sexuality *and the Colonial Order of Things*. Durham, N.C.: Duke University Press, 1995.

Stryker, Susan, ed. *The Transgender Issue.* Special issue. *GLQ: A Journal of Lesbian and Gay Studies* 4 (1998).

Todorov, Tzvetan. *La conquête de l'Amérique.* Paris: Seuil, 1982.

———. *The Conquest of America: The Question of the Other.* Translated by Richard Howard. 1985. Reprint, New York: Harper & Row, 1992.

Traub, Valerie. "The (In)Significance of 'Lesbian' Desire in Early Modern England." In *Queering the Renaissance,* edited by Jonathan Goldberg, 62–83. Durham, N.C.: Duke University Press, 1994.

———. "The Renaissance of Lesbianism in Early Modern England." *GLQ: A Journal of Lesbian and Gay Studies* 7 (2001): 245–63.

———. *The Renaissance of Lesbianism in Early Modern England.* Cambridge: Cambridge University Press, 2002.

Trexler, Richard. *Sex and Conquest: Gendered Violence, Political Order, and the European Conquest of the Americas.* Ithaca, N.Y.: Cornell University Press, 1995.

Van Den Abbeele, Georges. *Travel as Metaphor from Montaigne to Rousseau.* Minneapolis: University of Minnesota Press, 1992.

Vickers, Nancy. "Vital Signs: Petrarch and Popular Culture." *Romanic Review* 79 (1988): 184–95.

Wallace, David. "Carving Up Time and the World: Medieval-Renaissance Turf Wars." *Historiography and Personal History,* Working Paper No. 11. University of Wisconsin, Milwaukee, Center for Twentieth Century Studies, 1990–91.

———. *Chaucerian Polity: Absolutist Lineages and Associational Forms in England and Italy.* Stanford, Calif.: Stanford University Press, 1997.

Walters, Jonathan. " 'No More Than a Boy': The Shifting Construction of Masculinity from Ancient Greece to the Middle Ages." *Gender and History* 5 (1993): 20–33.

Warner, Michael. "Homo-Narcissism; or, Heterosexuality." In *Engendering Men: The Question of Male Feminist Criticism,* edited by Joseph A. Boone and Michael Cadden, 190–206. New York: Routledge, 1990.

———, ed. *Fear of a Queer Planet: Queer Politics and Social Theory.* Minneapolis: University of Minnesota Press, 1993.

———, ed. *Queer Transexions of Race, Nation, and Gender.* Special issue. *Social Text* 52/53 (1997): 3–4.

Weber, Samuel. *Institution and Interpretation: Expanded Edition.* Stanford, Calif.: Stanford University Press, 2001.

White, Hayden. *Metahistory: The Historical Imagination in Nineteenth-Century Europe.* Baltimore: Johns Hopkins University Press, 1973.

———. "Historical Text as Literary Artifact." In *The Writing of History:*

Literary Form and Historical Understanding, edited by R. H. Canary, 41–62. Madison: University of Wisconsin Press, 1978.

Wiegman, Robyn. "Feminism, Institutionalism, and the Idiom of Failure." *Differences: A Journal of Feminist Cultural Studies* 11.3 (1999): 107–36.

———. "What Ails Feminist Criticism? A Second Opinion." *Critical Inquiry* 25.2 (1999): 362–79.

Wolf, Eric R. *Europe and the People without History*. Berkeley: University of California Press, 1982.

Zavarzadeh, Mas'ud, Teresa L. Ebert, and Donald Morton, eds. *Marxism, Queer Theory, Gender*. Syracuse, N.Y.: Red Factory, 2001.

Žižek, Slavoj. *Looking Awry: An Introduction to Jacques Lacan through Popular Culture*. Cambridge: MIT Press, 1991.

———. "Melancholy and the Act." *Critical Inquiry* 26 (2000): 657–81.

Index

CARLA FRECCERO is the chair of the Department of Literature and a professor of literature, history of consciousness, and women's studies at the University of California, Santa Cruz. She is the author of *Popular Culture: An Introduction* and *Father Figures: Genealogy and Narrative Structure in Rabelais* and a coeditor of *Premodern Sexualities*.